RISK, REGULATION, AND
INVESTOR PROTECTION

RISK, REGULATION, AND INVESTOR PROTECTION

THE CASE OF INVESTMENT MANAGEMENT

JULIAN FRANKS
AND
COLIN MAYER

CLARENDON PRESS · OXFORD

1989

Oxford University Press, Walton Street, Oxford OX2 6DP
Oxford New York Toronto
Delhi Bombay Calcutta Madras Karachi
Petaling Jaya Singapore Hong Kong Tokyo
Nairobi Dar es Salaam Cape Town
Melbourne Auckland
and associated companies in
Berlin Ibadan

Oxford is a trade mark of Oxford University Press

Published in the United States
by Oxford University Press, New York

British Library Cataloguing in Publication Data
Franks, Julian
Risks, regulation, and investor protection: the case
of investment management.
1. Investment. Risks. Management
I. Title II. Mayer, C. P. (Colin P.)
332.6
ISBN 0–19–823315–9

Library of Congress Cataloging in Publication Data
Franks, Julian R.
Risk, regulation, and investor protection: the case of investment
management / Julian Franks and Colin Mayer.
Includes bibliographical references.
1. Investment advisors—Great Britain. 2. Securities industry-
-Great Britain. 3. Securities fraud—Great Britain—Case studies.
I. Mayer, C. P. (Colin P.) II. Title.
HG5432.F73 1989   332.6'0941—dc20   89–39349
ISBN 0–19–823315–9

Set by Hope Services (Abingdon) Ltd
Printed in Great Britain by
Courier International Ltd.
Tiptree, Essex

To our wives

Preface

In November 1982, the Investment Management Regulatory Organization (IMRO) commissioned a study of IMRO's capital requirements. The terms of reference of the study were 'to conduct research into IMRO's capital adequacy requirements and to make recommendations as to such changes as [were thought] appropriate to IMRO's present rules in this respect'. This book reports the results of that investigation.

In undertaking this study, we have sought advice and evidence from numerous quarters. Throughout the investigation we have been guided by a steering group established by IMRO. Members of the group included Christine Downton (County Natwest Capital Markets Ltd), Harold Littlefair, John Morgan (IMRO), George Ritchie (Freshfields), Keith Robinson (IMRO), Ronald Smith (IMRO), Andrew Thrall (SIB), Andrew Threadgold (Postel Investment Management Ltd), and Kenneth West (Prudential Portfolio Managers Ltd). We are especially grateful to John Morgan (Chief Executive, IMRO) who chaired the meetings of the steering committee and commented in detail on several drafts of the report, and to Keith Robinson, who spent considerable amounts of time discussing the study and providing contacts with other IMRO members and organizations. We also wish to thank Ron Smith for guiding us through IMRO's inspection procedures.

An important part of the study was the survey of IMRO members. Representatives of more than twenty institutions kindly agreed to be interviewed, some more than once. We are grateful for the time that members gave us. Another forty IM firms completed lengthy questionnaires which provided valuable information for the report.

Many other organizations assisted us. They included the Bank of England, the Department of Trade and Industry, the Fraud Squad, the Office of Fair Trading, the Securities and Exchange Commission, the Securities and Investments Board, the Stock Exchange Council, and the United Trust Association.

Professor Harold Rose read the entire manuscript and provided valuable comments. Several students provided useful research assistance for Chapters 2, 3, and 4. They included Anil Currimjee, Mary D'Arcy Doherty, and Rama Sundaram. Nicholas Carrick and Keith Lloyd also helped us with Chapter 4. Finally, we are grateful to Suzanne Hore for her excellent typing of the report.

The opinions expressed in this report are those of the authors and do not necessarily reflect those of the sponsoring organization or any institution with which the authors are associated.

Contents

Contents

List of Figures

List of Tables

Terms of Reference of the Report

1   to examine the reasons why an investment manager should hold capital;

2   to analyse the risk involved in investment management;

3   to identify the risks in 2 above for which an appropriate safeguard would be capital of some kind;

4   to consider the various types of allowable capital and the amount of each type which an IMRO member should hold;

5   in so far as is practical, to compare the recommendations arising from 1–4 above with what actually happens in practice;

6   by reference to the scope of IMRO's membership, to analyse what exceptions to the general capital adequacy requirements should be made with regard to any specific category of member;

7   to assess, in the light of 1–6 above, whether IMRO's current capital adequacy rules should be changed and if so in what respect.

1 Introduction

SECTION 1   The Background To and Purpose Of the Report

1.1   This report investigates capital requirements for investment managers. It was commissioned by the Investment Management Regulatory Organization (IMRO) as part of an exercise to evaluate IMRO's capital requirements.

1.2   The study was performed during 1988. It took place against the background of substantial changes: the implementation of the Financial Services Act in April 1988, fundamental changes to the structure of financial services in London, the October 1987 stock market crash, and the prospect of further changes arising from the dismantling of barriers to the free flow of capital and financial services in the EEC in 1992. There was therefore considerable uncertainty about the direction in which financial services were moving and much debate about the appropriate form that investor protection should take in the UK and elsewhere.

1.3   A central focus of discussion involved rules relating to capital requirements imposed on financial institutions. Section 49 of the Financial Services Act states that 'The Secretary of State may make rules requiring persons authorized to carry on investment business by virtue of sections 25 or 31 above to have and maintain in respect of that business such financial resources as are required by the rules', and furthermore that the rules under this section may 'make provision as to assets, liabilities and other matters to be taken into account in determining a person's financial resources for the purposes of the rules and the extent to which and the manner in which they are to be taken into account for that purpose'.

1.4   There is, therefore, a presumption in investor protection legislation in the UK that capital should be required of financial institutions. A marked distinction is drawn between the financial sector and most other sectors of the British economy, in which there are no equivalent requirements. What, if anything, differentiates financial services is an issue that this report has to address as part of the process of evaluating current requirements.

1.5 The authorities responded to this legislation by setting up the Securities and Investments Board (SIB) and a number of 'self-regulating organizations' (SROs). Under severe time restraints laid down by the legislation, a comprehensive set of rules was introduced.

1.6 There is a large literature on why capital should be required of banks and how those capital requirements should be determined. That literature is reviewed in Chapter 5. A distinction is, however, frequently drawn between banks and non-banks on several accounts. First, banks are viewed as playing a pivotal role in the functioning of an economy by providing transaction services (i.e. monetary liabilities), which facilitate the exchange of goods and services, and by transforming short-term liabilities (deposits) into long-term assets (loans). Second, unlike banks, investment managers do not have fixed liabilities, save in circumstances in which payments (such as pensions) are guaranteed. They simply manage portfolios whose values may increase or diminish without imposing any risk of default or bankruptcy on the investment manager. Third, and following from this, non-banks are not prone to the runs that may afflict banks. Since the liquidation of banks' assets in general falls well short of their liabilities, there is an ever-present risk that depositors, who are unsecured claimants on a bank, may withdraw their funds simply in response to a real or imaginary threat that other depositors will do likewise. The liquidation value of clients' funds in investment managers is not affected in the same way by the behaviour of other investors. Thus, while capital is required to discourage runs on banks, an equivalent need may not arise in investment management.

1.7 Broker/dealers are also thought to play a central role in the functioning of a financial system. IMRO's current rule book in large part reflects an extrapolation of the rules pertaining to broker/dealers. Capital is required of broker/dealers, so a similar requirement was thought to be necessary for investment managers. However, since the risks in investment management are not the same as those in broking and dealing, a different set of rules was implemented. Nevertheless, the principle that capital should be required of investment managers has not been questioned.

1.8 Is the analogy with broker/dealers or banks appropriate? To answer that question, we have to go through three stages of analysis. First, we have to establish what the risks are to the investor in the investment management business. Second, we have to determine the extent to which these risks give rise to a need for public intervention in the form of capital requirements or the regulation of other activities of investment managers. Economic theory suggests that, where markets are imperfect (for example where investors are inadequately informed) and risks are not appropriately priced, a need for regulation may exist. These market imperfections are said to create a 'market failure', and market failures provide a prima facie case for regulation. Where market failures cannot be established, regulation is not warranted. The form that such regulation should take, and in particular the role of capital, constitutes the third part of the investigation.

SECTION 2 The Structure of the Report

2.1 The report begins in *Chapter 2* with a description of the investment management business. It describes the structure of the industry, the different types of firms operating in the industry, and the investments made by its participants. It discusses the way in which the investment management function is conducted and the process by which transactions are settled in the UK. This is illustrated in some detail in relation to one type of investment management firm—unit trusts.

2.2 *Chapter 3* then considers the risks associated with these investment management functions. It distinguishes between non-financial risks associated with the investment process and financial risks resulting from operating and capital gearing. It discusses the extent to which these risks may impinge on the investor. This chapter draws heavily on interviews that were conducted with investment managers and the results of a survey. It also examines evidence from share price data on the risk of investment management firms.

2.3 *Chapter 4* discusses recent examples of investment managers in the UK who have encountered problems. It considers cases where the cause of failure has been fraud, negligence, or pure financial risk. Five classes of loss are considered: (a) employee fraud against the firm, (b) theft of client funds, (c) irregular dealing, (d) companies set up to defraud, and (e) pure financial failure. Seven cases of fraud and financial distress are described in detail in the Appendix, and lessons are drawn from these cases for the design of investor protection.

2.4 *Chapter 5* surveys the relevant academic literature. While there are no existing studies of capital requirements for non-banks, there are several related literatures. The first is on corporate capital structures; the second is on capital requirements for banks; and the third is on regulating the professions.

2.5 The case for capital requirements is examined in *Chapter 6*, which is in eight sections. Section 2 lists the risks to investors in the investment management business that were described in detail in Chapters 3 and 4. Section 3 examines whether there are any market failures that arise from these risks that may give rise to a prima facie case for regulation. Section 4 broadens the analysis to take account of systemic risks.

2.6 Section 5 of Chapter 6 describes alternative methods of correcting market failures, and Section 6 considers the merits and deficiencies of each. This lays the foundation in Section 7 for relating the market failures of Sections 3 and 4 to the different forms of investor protection described in Section 6. Finally, Section 8 summarizes the main recommendations.

2.7 *Chapter 7* describes current IMRO rules on capital requirements. These are analysed in the context of the framework
discussed in the previous chapter. In particular, their ability to
correct market failures and provide effective but low-cost investor
protection is assessed. Problems in both the principles underlying
current rules and their precise specification are discussed and
proposals for changes are made. The chapter also describes
regulation of investment management firms in the USA. This
provides an opportunity to compare both existing UK regulations
and recommendations in this report with the US regulatory
system.

2.8 *Chapter 8*, the last chapter, draws together the analysis in this
report. It summarizes the criteria that should be used in identifying
appropriate forms of investor protection, the evidence on the
nature and scale of risks that investors face, and the choices
available to regulators. Finally, it describes the structure of
regulation suggested by this analysis.

2 The Investment Management Business

SECTION 1 Introduction

1.1 Wiley's *Dictionary of Banking* defines investment management as

a service entailing the management of an investment portfolio on behalf of a private client or an institution, the receipt and distribution of dividends and all other administrative work in connection with the portfolio. These investment 'accounts', as they are usually called, may be conducted on either a discretionary basis (in which case the investment manager acts at his own discretion in the management of a portfolio, without referring to the client) or non-discretionary basis (in which case the manager will recommend investment sales and purchases to the client and await the latter's approval).

1.2 For our purposes, investment management will be defined more widely than this to include firms that are acting in a purely advisory capacity. Within the terms of the Financial Services Act we are therefore primarily concerned with Schedule 1, paragraph 14 ('Managing investments'), Schedule 1, paragraph 15 ('Investment advice'), and Schedule 1, paragraph 16 ('Establishing, operating or winding up a collective investment scheme, including acting as trustee of an authorised unit trust scheme').

1.3 Investment management originated as a service for private clients. The first investment trusts were established in Scotland in the middle of the nineteenth century with the aim of affording investors of moderate means the superior returns from pooled interests in shares of joint-stock companies. Initially, the clearing banks were instrumental in expanding the investment management business. Subsequently, merchant banks and stockbrokers and, more recently, specialist fund managers have come to dominate the industry. Furthermore, taxation has encouraged the growth of financial intermediaries, so that now a substantial proportion of investment services are provided for institutional rather than private clients.

1.4 The purpose of this chapter is to identify the type of investor involved in the investment management process. The risks borne may depend upon whether the investor is an institution, say a pension fund, or an individual. As a consequence, *caveat emptor* may be felt to be more appropriate for one class of investor than another.

1.5 The risks borne by the investor in the investment management (IM) process may depend upon the types of securities purchased. Settlement delays will be much less important in transactions involving gilts than shares, since the settlement period is two days for the former and up to ten working days for the latter. Unit trust investments may be better protected against fraud than other funds. One reason is that, by law, clients' securities and cash balances must be strictly separated from the investment manager and held by a (regulated) trustee. In contrast, such strict separation has not been imposed on the rest of the IM industry.

1.6 The chapter is in six sections. Section 2 describes the structure of the investment management industry. It records the sizes of different sectors, their asset allocations, and the division between domestic and overseas investments. Section 3 examines the investment management function, the fee structure of the industry, and the difference between discretionary and non-discretionary investments.

1.7 The investment management process and the process by which transactions are settled is described in Section 4.

1.8 One sector of investment management that requires further analysis is the unit trust business. This raises particular complications because of the nature of the service provided (the creation and redemption of units) and the tripartite relation that exists between the unit trust, the investment manager, and the trustee. Unit trusts illustrate the different investment management functions rather clearly and so are examined in greater detail in Section 5.

1.9   Section 6 summarizes the major implications of this analysis for the subsequent examination of the risks of the investment management business and the protection that should be afforded to the investor.

SECTION 2   The Investment Management Industry

Part A   The Sectors

2.1   There are four major institutional sectors in the investment management (hereafter IM) industry. These are:

- life insurance companies;
- investment trusts;
- pension funds;
- unit trusts.

Two other major classes of investor are charities and private clients.

2.2   By the end of 1986, the combined assets of the four major types of institution listed above were £401 billion. To put this in context, at the end of 1986 the assets of building societies were £117 billion, while the sterling liabilities of UK banks were £296 billion, and their total assets were £907 billion.

2.3   Table 2.1 records the assets managed by the four institutional sectors over the period 1981–6. The lower half of the table reports assets as a percentage of the total value of assets managed by institutions. The largest single group is pension funds; they account for nearly half of total institutional assets under management. Not far behind are insurance companies, with about 40 per cent of assets under management. Investment and unit trusts hold just over 10 per cent of assets. However, while comparatively small in terms of asset shares, unit trusts and investment trusts together still held over £50 billion of assets on behalf of clients in 1986. Furthermore, unit trusts have been enjoying a rapid growth in activity that has nearly doubled their share of the market from 4 to 8 per cent over just five years.[1]

Table 2.1 The UK investment management industry, assets managed, 1981–1986

	1981	1982	1983	1984	1985	1986
	(£m)					
Insurance companies	61,084	79,868	95,913	113,561	130,122	158,551
Investment trusts	8,904	10,051	13,371	15,251	18,085	20,468
Pension funds	63,306	84,075	106,074	134,071	156,082	189,925
Unit trusts	5,621	7,489	11,289	14,797	19,258	31,662
TOTAL	138,915	181,483	226,647	277,680	323,547	400,606
	(%)					
Insurance companies	44.0	44.0	42.3	40.9	40.2	39.6
Investment trusts	6.4	5.5	5.9	5.5	5.6	5.1
Pension funds	45.6	46.3	46.8	48.3	48.2	47.4
Unit trusts	4.0	4.2	5.0	5.3	6.0	7.9
TOTAL*	100.0	100.0	100.0	100.0	100.0	100.0

* Because of rounding, these numbers may not sum to 100.

Source: CSO, *Financial Statistics*.

2.4 This last point is seen more clearly in Table 2.2, which records the growth rate of assets under management. The table shows an average growth of total assets under management by institutions of around 22 per cent per annum over the period. This compares with an average annual growth of 21.7 per cent in the FT All Share Index and 5.5 per cent in the Retail Price Index. But over the same period, unit trust assets expanded by an average of 40 per cent per annum.

[1] The effect of the stock market crash on unit trust activity is discussed in the next chapter.

Table 2.2 Growth rates of assets under management by UK institution, 1982–1986 (%)

	1982	1983	1984	1985	1986
Growth in total institutional assets	30.6	24.9	22.5	16.5	23.8
Growth in insurance companies' assets	30.8	20.1	18.4	14.6	21.9
Growth in investment trust assets	12.9	33.0	14.1	18.6	13.2
Growth in pension fund assets	32.8	26.2	26.4	16.4	21.7
Growth in unit trust assets	33.2	50.7	31.1	30.1	64.4
Memoranda items					
Increase in Retail Price Index (RPI)	8.6	4.6	5.0	6.1	3.5
Increase in Financial Times All Share Index (FT 500)	15.6	26.5	19.0	23.5	24.1

Source: CSO, *Financial Statistics* and *Economic Trends*.

2.5 The very large presence of institutions in the IM business may well affect the design of investor protection. We pursue this issue below. In interpreting the data presented here, it should be borne in mind that investing institutions are frequently 'connected' to (i.e. are part of the same legal entity as) investment managers. In such cases assets under management will include in-house investments as well as those managed for external clients.

Part B   The Assets

2.6   Table 2.3 records the division of institutional assets between domestic and overseas holdings. It shows that the proportion of assets held overseas increased from 11 per cent in 1981 to 19 per cent in 1986.

2.7   Tables 2.4 and 2.5 disaggregate domestic and overseas portfolios into short-term assets, government securities, corporate securities, unit trust units, property, and 'other' by value (Table 2.4) and percentages (Table 2.5). The largest class of asset held is domestic corporate equity. This accounted for over 50 per cent of

Table 2.3 Portfolio allocation of UK institutions between domestic and overseas assets, 1981–1986

	1981	1982	1983	1984	1985	1986
	(£m)					
Domestic	123,606	157,931	190,448	233,137	271,574	325,593
Overseas	15,347	24,675	36,367	44,874	54,286	75,663
TOTAL*	138,953	182,606	226,815	278,011	325,860	401,256
	(% of total assets)					
Domestic	89.0	87.0	84.0	83.9	83.9	81.4
Overseas	11.0	13.0	16.0	16.1	16.1	18.6
TOTAL	100.0	100.0	100.0	100.0	100.0	100.0

* Because of revisions, these numbers may not be exactly the same as in Table 2.1.

Source: CSO, *Financial Statistics*.

domestic assets by the end of the period and recorded a remarkable growth of 12 per cent of the share of total assets over the five years from 1981 to 1986. The proportion of overseas assets held as equities was even higher at around 90 per cent, and, given the substantial increase in overseas holdings, overseas equities rose as a proportion of total assets held.

2.8 The growth in equities' share occurred at the expense of a declining share of property investments, which fell from 24 to 13 per cent of assets held, and of UK government securities.

2.9 Table 2.6 demonstrates that the previous tables hide substantial variations in portfolio allocations across institutions. Insurance companies and pension funds are much more heavily concentrated in domestic assets than investment and unit trusts. Investment and unit trusts hold a large proportion of their domestic assets in equities. Pension funds have much larger equity holdings (as a proportion of total assets) than insurance companies.

Both have larger gilt and property holdings than investment and unit trusts.

2.10 The next chapter will present evidence on the way in which risks associated with the investment management process depend on the nature and location of assets held. For example, settlement problems will be seen to have been more acute in some overseas markets than in the domestic one; there are more errors and delays in equity than in gilt transactions; and there are particular problems associated with the pricing of unit trust units. It may therefore be thought that differences in the composition of institutions' portfolios should be reflected in regulatory requirements. This issue is pursued in Chapters 6 and 7 when discussing the relation between risks and investor protection.

Table 2.4 Portfolio allocation of UK institutions by asset, 1981–1986 (£m)

	1981	1982	1983	1984	1985	1986
Domestic						
Short-term assets	3,909	4,723	6,489	7,856	8,790	10,409
UK govt. securities	28,088	41,552	48,276	52,989	58,676	61,523
Corporate sec.—equity	52,421	66,957	84,931	112,670	139,185	176,987
Corporate sec.—other	3,413	4,371	5,408	6,388	7,060	9,391
Unit trust units	2,096	2,893	4,644	6,603	9,211	14,033
Property	29,572	32,330	34,329	37,521	39,966	43,033
Other	4,107	5,105	6,371	9,110	8,686	10,217
DOMESTIC TOTAL	123,606	157,931	190,448	233,137	271,574	325,593
Overseas						
Short-term assets	364	1,868	1,280	2,303	1,645	2,812
Govt. securities	237	836	819	1,358	1,606	3,023
Corporate sec.—equity	13,969	20,813	32,761	39,276	48,836	66,932
Other	777	1,158	1,507	1,937	2,199	2,896
OVERSEAS TOTAL	15,347	24,675	36,367	44,874	54,286	75,663
TOTAL	138,953	182,606	226,815	278,011	325,860	401,256

Source: CSO, *Financial Statistics*.

Table 2.5 Portfolio allocation of UK institutions by asset, 1981–1986 (%)

	1981	1982	1983	1984	1985	1986
Domestic						
Short-term assets	3.2	3.0	3.4	3.4	3.2	3.2
UK govt. securities	22.7	26.3	25.3	22.7	21.6	18.9
Corporate sec.—equity	42.4	42.4	44.6	48.3	51.3	54.4
Corporate sec.—other	2.8	2.8	2.8	2.7	2.6	2.9
Unit trust units	1.7	1.8	2.4	2.8	3.4	4.3
Property	23.9	20.5	18.0	16.1	14.7	13.2
Other	3.3	3.2	3.4	3.9	3.2	3.1
DOMESTIC TOTAL*	100.0	100.0	99.9	99.9	100.0	100.0
Overseas						
Short-term assets	2.4	7.6	3.5	5.1	3.0	3.7
Govt. securities	1.5	3.4	2.3	3.0	3.0	4.0
Corporate sec.—equity	91.0	84.3	90.1	87.5	90.0	88.5
Other	5.1	4.7	4.1	4.3	4.1	3.8
OVERSEAS TOTAL*	100.0	100.0	100.0	99.9	100.1	100.0

* Because of rounding, these numbers may not sum to 100.

Source: CSO, *Financial Statistics*.

SECTION 3   The Investment Management Function

3.1   An investment manager can act in a number of capacities. At one extreme, investment managers can provide advice to clients on portfolio allocations. This service is termed *advice only*. The investment manager has no discretion over the management of clients' funds. At the other extreme, investment managers have full power of attorney to manage clients' portfolios at their discretion. Larger investment managers frequently have a policy of only managing clients' portfolios on a *full discretionary basis*.

3.2 The management of clients' investments and the advice offered to investors will be based on *research* provided by in-house teams or outside brokers. Since UK equities tend to be comprehensively analysed by stockbrokers, in-house research teams often concentrate on other types of investment and overseas markets. Proprietary information is an important source of product differentiation and competitive advantage for an investment manager.

Table 2.6 Portfolio allocation of different institutions in 1986 (%)

	Insurance companies	Investment trusts	Pension funds	Unit trusts
Domestic	87.0	49.1	82.6	60.2
Overseas	13.0	50.9	17.4	39.8
TOTAL	100.0	100.0	100.0	100.0
Domestic				
Short-term assets	5.3*	2.9†	4.2*	5.7†
UK govt. securities	22.9	3.0	18.9	2.8
Corporate sec.—equity	38.0	86.3	62.3	86.1
Corporate sec.—other	3.9	3.6	1.5	5.0
Unit trust units	8.3	2.7	0.8	—
Property	14.6	0.4	9.0	—
Other	7.1	1.0	3.5	0.4
DOMESTIC TOTAL	100.1	99.9	100.2	100.0
Overseas				
Short-term assets	2.3*	1.3†	1.7*	2.5†
Govt. securities	18.4	4.5	3.5	—
Corporate sec.—equity	71.1	87.0	92.7	93.1
Other	8.3	7.2	2.1	4.4
OVERSEAS TOTAL	100.1	100.0	100.0	100.0

* Gross.   † Net.

Source: CSO, *Financial Statistics*, 1988.

3.3 Where discretion is granted, investment managers are responsible for the management of clients' portfolios. This requires that investment managers initiate transactions and oversee their subsequent *execution*. Thus, managers place orders with brokers or dealers for the sale and purchase of securities and then monitor the subsequent transactions through to settlement. Where errors have occurred on account of a failure of managers, say, to adhere to guidelines stipulated by clients, or because of the initiation of incorrect transactions or inadequate monitoring, then the manager is responsible for rectifying these errors.

3.4 Investment managers may assume broader responsibilities. Once an order has been placed with a broker or dealer, the subsequent execution and settlement is no longer under the direct control of the investment manager. However, in practice it is frequently difficult to assign responsibility for the different stages of the investment management process. Instead then of restricting management to the initiation of transactions, investment managers often assume responsibility for the *broking* and *settling* of transactions. Thus, incorrect purchases and sales and delays in settlement may, at least in the first instance, create liabilities for investment managers, although compensation may be sought from other parties. Furthermore, brokers, dealers and managers may well be part of the same legal entity, so that the dividing line between management, broking and settling functions may only be a reflection of organizational arrangements. Mistakes made by the broking or banking arm of a financial institution will create losses for a group of which the investment manager is a part. It may be harder to substantiate 'best' practice in circumstances in which in-house brokers and dealers are employed. Investment managers may well feel more impelled to pay compensation in circumstances in which in-house brokerage and market-making functions are employed.

3.5 Investment managers may have *custody* (power of attorney) over clients' securities and monies. Custody of clients' accounts may be conferred irrespective of whether clients' accounts are separated from those of the firm. There are three forms in which clients' monies may be held: (a) the firm's own account, (b) a group client account, and (c) individual client accounts. Where the investment manager is part of a group that is a licensed deposit-taker, the accounts may be held within the same group.

3.6 Under the Financial Services Act, clients' accounts have to be separated from those of the investment manager. But the investment manager may, and frequently in the case of discretionary management will, retain control of clients' accounts. As a result, separation does not usually mean loss of control. The investment manager is then responsible for the proper handling of clients' accounts.

3.7 The investment manager will be responsible for ensuring that securities are properly registered and accounts maintained. The *administrative function* may encompass other activities, such as the preparation of statements for tax authorities.

3.8 To summarize, the investment management function will frequently involve activities that are associated with brokers, dealers, and banks as well as the proffering of advice and the managing of clients' portfolios. As a consequence, the risks associated with the investment management process may include those of the broking function (such as settlement and counterparty risks), the dealing function (position risk), and the banking function (the holding of clients' securities and monies).

3.9 A typical schedule of fees is as follows.

Service	Fee
Management fee	0.5 per cent on first £5 million under management, based on market value; beyond £5 million a fee of 0.15 per cent; any purchases of in-house unit trusts are excluded from the fee.
Transactions	No fee if transaction is direct with market maker; fee of 0.2 per cent with agency broker; no fee on gilts

3.10 There are significant variations in the base on which charges are levied. In many cases, fees are levied as a percentage of the previous quarter's market value of funds under management. In other cases, the valuation refers to an earlier period or to an average of valuations over a number of previous periods. The significance of this stems from the fact that the volatility of fee income will be crucially dependent on the basis on which charges are levied: firms that set fees in relation to an average of past valuations did not feel the full impact of the 1987 stock market crash for some time.

3.11   There are also differences in the extent to which services are separately charged. Some clients demand transparency in pricing; others, for reasons associated with internal accounting conventions, prefer charges to be subsumed under a total management fee. The significance of this stems from the incentives that different pricing systems give managers to pursue certain practices (for example, the 'churning' of clients' accounts: see ch. 4, para. 2.16). Transparency may permit more precise identification of the pricing of particular services but may encourage the over-provision of services whose prices exceed their marginal cost of provision.

SECTION 4   The Investment Management Process

4.1   It will be assumed in the following discussion of the investment management process that the investment manager is acting for the client on a full discretionary basis.

4.2   The investment manager will instruct by telephone (usually through the IM firm's dealer if it is an integrated investment house) an agency broker or market-maker to execute a transaction. The telephone order to the agency broker or market-maker will include the name of the security, the size of the order, and any price limits.

4.3   Details of bargains are reported by both brokers and counter-parties to the Checking System of the Stock Exchange on a daily basis. The Checking System matches transactions by value, security numbers, and counterparties. Only matched bargains are passed on to the Stock Exchange's central computer system, TALISMAN, where they form the basis for settlement. One source in the Stock Exchange estimated that up to 10 per cent of transactions are mismatched and disallowed by the Checking System.

4.4 The order will be checked at the end of the day by the IM firm's dealer with the broker or market-maker. The IM manager will receive a contract note for the transaction, and an advice note will be sent to the client for his or her share of the transaction. The client's order for a particular security will frequently be part of a larger order for the security. If the full order cannot be executed, some apportionment must take place and the apportionment must conform to 'best practice'.

4.5 Prior to entry to TALISMAN, a streaming of transactions occurs where only UK-equity-related transactions are passed on. Transactions relating to gilts are referred to the Bank of England, and US securities are directed to the International Securities Clearing Corporation in New York or the Midwest Clearing Corporation in Chicago.

4.6 Members of the Stock Exchange that are selling stock on behalf of IM firms or their clients deposit stock with the Stock Exchange where it is transferred into the Exchange's nominee company, SEPON. The physical stock is then sent for registration out of the seller's name into SEPON. This process has the advantage of protecting the sellers' interest until settlement takes place. Thus, even if the broker through whom the securities were sold goes bankrupt, the seller does not suffer since the securities are in the safe custody of the Stock Exchange (see Figure 2.1). Settlement of sold bargains is effected by a book entry transfer of ownership of stock within TALISMAN. All stock in the process of settlement is held in uncertified form in the nominee company SEPON.

4.7 Every member-firm who acts as a principal has a trading account within TALISMAN for every security they deal in. They

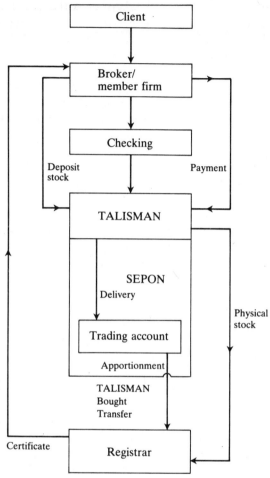

Fig. 2.1 The settlement process

may hold stock in their trading account and give instructions to withdraw it or use it to settle bargains when they have in turn sold stock. Principal sold bargains awaiting apportionment are placed in a queue. Stock in the trading account is apportioned to all principal sold bargains by book entry transfer until either no stock is left or all outstanding bargains have been fulfilled.

4.8 In the case of a bargain where stock is due to be delivered to a client, a TALISMAN Bought Transfer is prepared showing the details of the buying client. This is sent to the registrar, who then registers stock out of SEPON into the buyer's name.

4.9 Certificates are produced by registrars and issued to member-firms for onward transmission to their clients. All payments due to and from each member-firm are netted into one figure for each firm.

4.10 Share transactions are settled at the end of the Stock Exchange Account (usually fortnightly). Gilts are settled within two days of transaction. Settlement involves an exchange of cash for the securities (i.e. share certificates). One exception is a purchase of a new issue, where cash is paid without contemporaneous receipt of securities. The longer the settlement period, the more exposed investors are to losses from a counterparty default.

4.11 Settlement may be delayed because the securities or the cash are not available. The former is more usual than the latter. Securities may be unavailable because of back office problems at another brokerage firm or because of administrative delays at the company's registrar, or because the security has been lost. In that event, cash payment will invariably be delayed. If settlement is delayed, an interest saving will accrue for a purchase transaction, whereas in a sale there is an interest loss. IM firms differ in their response to such delays. In some cases client accounts are credited or debited by the IM firm on settlement day, regardless of the date of physical settlement. Other firms debit and credit clients on the basis of physical settlement. Discussions with IM managers suggest that the former is more prevalent.

4.12 The fortnightly settlement also introduces the possibility of member-firm or counter-party default. To combat risks arising from this process, the Stock Exchange has instituted two risk management facilities: the Stock Note Service and the Institutional Net Settlement Service.

4.13   As mentioned above, stock is apportioned out of a member-firm's trading account. The Stock Note Service provides institutions with an assurance from the Stock Exchange that, even if the member-firm through whom the securities were purchased defaults, stock will be dispatched for registration.

4.14   The Stock Note Service is available only to institutions that notify member-firms that they wish to avail themselves of it. The Exchange does not guarantee the transaction; all it provides is an assurance that stock will be despatched for registration even if the member-firm does not have sufficient securities in its trading account. As yet, this system has never been tested.

4.15   In July 1988, the Stock Exchange introduced the Institutional Net Settlement Service (INSS). This is a centralized system which allows member-firms and institutions to settle their transactions on a net basis across the market.

4.16   Under the old system, settlements were done with member-firms on a net basis; settlements were treated at arm's length through member-firms. Under INSS, the intervening layer of member-firms is dispensed with and institutions can deal directly with the Exchange. This is expected to reduce appreciably the risk of counter-party default.

4.17   To date, the main source of protection for investors has been the Stock Exchange Compensation Fund. This provided for a maximum payout of up to £250,000 per private investor in the event of losses caused by default of a member-firm of the Exchange. According to Stock Exchange sources, there has been only one case (Giles & Overbury) of default by a member-firm in the last three years; the Stock Exchange Compensation Fund paid £1 million to private investors affected by the bankruptcy of Giles & Overbury.

SECTION 5   The Unit Trust Business

Part A   The Structure of the Industry

5.1   The unit trust industry started in the 1930s. Its advantage over investment trusts was perceived to be that the management company made a market in the unit trusts, and that the prices of units bore a close and predetermined relation to the value of the underlying securities. Since then the unit trust market has grown enormously and, as previously described, expanded four-fold between 1982 and 1986 to £32 billion at end 1986.

5.2   The market for unit trusts is very competitive. At the end of 1986, there were 1,053 unit trusts managed by 167 fund management groups. Concentration is low and has decreased appreciably over recent years. The shares of the top five, ten, and fifteen funds measured by funds under management in 1984, 1985, and 1986 is shown in Table 2.7.

Table 2.7   Share of unit trust assets under management by the largest firms (%)

	1984	1985	1986
Top 5 firms	41.5	37.0	33.0
Top 10 firms	60.1	54.5	51.0
Top 15 firms	68.7	64.8	61.6

Source: James Capel.

5.3   Much of the change in industry structure over these years is attributable to the entry and expansion of the unit trust activities of insurance companies. As Table 2.8 records, in 1984 most unit trusts were independent of other financial groups; by 1986 the largest owners of unit trusts were insurance companies.

5.4   Ownership patterns may be relevant to the determination of capital requirements. Protection may be afforded to the unit trust operation by the capital and reputation of the parent. On the other

Table 2.8 Ownership of unit trust companies (% of assets under management)

	1984	1985	1986
Clearing banks	13.8	12.6	11.1
Independents	30.2	28.1	26.0
Independents with backing	10.5	9.5	8.6
Insurance companies	18.3	24.9	31.5
Merchant banks	21.8	20.6	18.6
Stockbrokers	4.3	4.1	4.1

Soure: James Capel.

hand, the operation of the unit trust may be jeopardized by the financial distress of the parent or related companies. We discuss such cases in subsequent chapters.

Part B   The Structure of a Unit Trust Firm

5.5   There are three distinct institutions involved in the activities of a unit trust. First, there is the *unit trust manager* himself. The unit trust manager defines the terms of the trust (i.e. the type of securities in which it invests), markets the unit trust, requests the trustee to create and redeem units, receives payments from investors, runs a 'box' (an inventory) of units, sends out unit trust certificates to investors, and appoints the trustee.

5.6   A 'recognized' *trustee* is appointed by the unit trust manager to protect the interests of investors. He receives payment from unit trust managers for the creation of units. The unit trust manager instructs the portfolio manager (who may be one and the same person) to purchase and sell securities that conform with the terms of the trust. It is the responsibility of the trustee to ensure that the terms are met in relation to purchases and sales of securities. The trustee owns and holds the securities in which the trust has invested on behalf of clients and also holds any uninvested cash. The trustees request the investment manager to provide valuations of the trust when units are created or redeemed, and it is the trustee's responsibility to ensure that adequate systems are employed for valuing funds. This custodianship function provides substantial protection against particular types of fraud.

5.7 The *investment manager* arranges for the purchase and sale of securities and for the provision of valuations for the trustee.

5.8 The unit trust manager and the investment manager may but need not be part of the same firm. The trustee is required to be a separate legal entity and must conform with particular legal requirements such as minimum capital requirements.

5.9 For reasons of economy, some unit trust managers delegate administrative functions, such as issuing contract notes, registering securities, and accounting to another unit trust management firm.

Part C   The Creation and Pricing of Units

5.10 When an investor subscribes to a unit trust, the money is sent to the unit trust manager. The unit trust manager credits the investor with units held in the 'box'. If no units are held or additional units are required for inventory purposes, the 'box' requests the trustee to create units. If units are to be created, the trustee in turn authorizes the investment manager to purchase the required volume of eligible securities that underlies the new units. The transaction is placed through a member of a recognized securities exchange. The settlement process was described in the previous section.

5.11 The price at which units are sold and redeemed depends on the value of the securities held in the unit trust. The trustee will request the investment manager to value the securities held at offer or bid price. The price of units is then computed by adding to the offer price stamp duty, stock broker's commission, VAT, dividends and interest receivable, and manager's charges. In total, the offer price of a unit could exceed the offer price of the underlying securities by 7.1 per cent, which, together with a dealing spread of 2 per cent, could give rise to a difference between unit offer and bid prices of 9.1 per cent. Figure 2.2 illustrates the determination of the pricing of units.

Maximum
offer
price

    Manager's charge ≈ 5.1%

    +

    Dividends + int. receivable

    +

    Stockbroker's commission + VAT 1.5%

    +

    Stamp duty $\frac{1}{2}$% (on purchases only)

    ————————— Valuation of units at offer price

Quoted bid
price

Minimum   ————————— Valuation of units at bid price
bid
price

Fig. 2.2   The pricing of unit trust units

5.12 Quoted spreads are normally much lower than this maximum permissible spread. Typically, during periods in which units are being created, the offer price of units will be set at the maximum permissible offer price and the bid price will be well above the true bid price of the underlying units. Quoted prices thus lie within the true bid–offer range. The quoted price will be equal to true offer during periods of net sales of units and will equal the bid price during periods of net redemptions. The prices at which the unit trust manager creates and cancels units with the trustee are the true bid and offer prices.

5.13 Traditionally, the price at which unit trust managers have transacted with investors has been the price associated with the last valuation of units—referred to as historic or *backward pricing*. Recently the Department of Trade and Industry has implemented new rules that give unit trust managers the choice of quoting prices on a forward or backward basis. The investor must be informed of the chosen method of pricing. *Forward pricing* means that units are sold at prices that prevail at the valuation (within hours of the order being processed). The advantage of forward pricing is that investors are sold units at (virtually) current rather than historic prices. The drawback is that investors do not know the transaction price when the order is placed. The concern has been expressed that this uncertainty will discourage investment in unit trusts.

5.14 Unit trust managers earn returns from two sources: management fees, and holding and dealing in units. Dealing gains arise from purchasing units at lower prices than the prices at which they are subsequently sold to investors. Holding gains relate to unrealized holdings of units held in the unit trust 'box'. The change from backward to forward pricing diminishes the possibility of earning profits on the 'box'.

5.15 Investment managers have been earning sizeable profits from dealing and holding gains on units. Table 2.9, column (3), records the fact that, in a sample of 25 unit trusts, 48 per cent of their total income in 1987 was derived from dealing and holding profits. This represented a return of nearly 1 per cent on the value of funds under management (col. (4)), and between 2 and 4 per cent of the value of sales and repurchases of units (cols. (1) and (2)). The second and third rows reveal a high degree of consistency in these estimates between firms with accounting year ends before and after the stock market crash. These dealing profits should have been reflected in lower commission rates charged to investors.

Table 2.9 Contribution of earnings from units to the total earnings of 25 unit trusts for accounting year 1987 (%)

	Dealing and holding profits on sale ÷ sales of units (1)	Dealing and holding profits on repurchases ÷ repurchases of units (2)	Dealing and holding profits on sales, repurchases, and liquidations ÷ total income of unit trusts (gross of expenses) (3)	Dealing and holding profits on sales, repurchases, and liquidations ÷ value of funds under m'gement (4)	Total profits (net of expenses) ÷ value of funds under m'gement (5)
Total sample	2.1	3.5	47.9	0.96	0.74
Firms with accounting year-ends before October 1987 (9 firms)	1.9	3.5	51.1	1.11	0.69
Firms with accounting year-ends after October 1987 (15 firms)	2.1	3.5	47.3	0.93	0.75

Source: Company accounts.

Part D   Summary of the Unit Trust Business

5.16   Unit trusts exemplify the different functions that investment mangers perform rather clearly. Unit trust managers act as dealers in taking positions in 'boxes' and as brokers in selling units to investors created by the trustee on behalf of the trust. Trustees act as custodians of securities for investors and undertake administration functions in keeping records of securities purchased and sold for the trust. Investment managers perform the portfolio management function in executing transactions on behalf of trustees.

5.17   The pricing of units raises particular problems associated with the valuation of funds under management. The use of historic (backward) pricing has permitted unit trust managers to earn profits from taking positions in the 'box' in excess of those resulting from the quoted spread. The change from backward to forward pricing is likely to diminish the opportunity for such gain appreciably. There is some evidence that fees are being raised to compensate, but declining profits, combined with reduced activity in the market after the stock market crash, is likely to result in a consolidation of firms within the unit trust business. It is unlikely therefore that the recent experience of diminishing market concentration will continue into the future.

5.18   The risks associated with profits on own positions in the 'box', the competitive nature of the unit trust business, and the interrelation between unit trust and other investment business bear closely on the appropriate design of investor protection and the appropriate level of capital requirements. Subsequent chapters explore the relation between risks and investor protection.

5.19   Since securities and cash balances are largely under the control of a custodian, the trustee, there is strict separation from the IM firm's funds. This strict separation is not a characteristic of the rest of the industry, where the IM firm (at least for discretionary funds) has control over both funds and securities.

SECTION 6   Summary of Chapter 2

6.1   There is a substantial institutional presence in the investment management business. Pension funds comprise the largest segment of the industry, but there has been a significant growth in unit trust activity.

6.2   At least until the crash, there was a steadily increasing proportion of overseas assets held in funds under management.

6.3   The prime form of security held by investment managers is equity. Overseas holdings are particularly heavily concentrated in equities.

6.4   Investment trusts and unit trusts hold a larger proportion of their assets overseas than pension funds and insurance companies.

6.5   Investment trusts and unit trusts hold a larger proportion of their assets in equities, and have fewer gilts and less property than pension funds and insurance companies.

6.6   Investment managers can act on a discretionary or non-discretionary basis. As an adjunct to the investment management process, they perform or are responsible for five functions in varying degrees of importance: execution, broking transactions, settling transactions, custody, and administration. The nature of the services provided determines the potential losses of investment managers.

6.7   Clients' funds can be held in group client accounts or individual client accounts. Under the Financial Services Act, they cannot be held in the firm's own account.

6.8   The unit trust business is highly competitive, with a low level of concentration.

6.9 The operation of a unit trust involves firms in broking, custody, investment management, and administrative functions. Unit trust managers effectively act as dealers in taking positions in 'boxes'.

6.10 Unit trust managers have earned a substantial proportion of their income from profits on the 'box' in the past.

6.11 The profits associated with these positions are closely related to the basis on which units are priced. The move to forward pricing is likely to diminish profits on the 'box' appreciably.

6.12 Stock Exchange systems offer some protection against risks of counterparty default. The fortnightly accounting period, however, often still leaves firms significantly exposed.

6.13 The trustee offers unit trust investors a substantial measure of protection that does not exist elsewhere in the investment management business.

3 Risks in the Investment Management Business and their Effect on Investors

SECTION 1   Introduction

1.1   This chapter investigates the risks born by an investor who employs an investment manager to manage or advise on the management of a portfolio. There are several different classes of risk that the investor faces. First and most obviously, the performance of the underlying assets reflects the quality of an investment manager's portfolio selection and an adviser's recommendations. However, unless minimum returns have been guaranteed or negligence can be demonstrated, the manager is not liable to the investor for under-performance. Comparative performance of investment managers is not therefore the proper subject of regulation and is not pursued here.

1.2   Second, the investor is exposed to loss if the investment management firm fails. This is the subject of a separate chapter (Chapter 4).

systemic /social risk

1.3   Third, there are risks arising from problems in the investment management process. There can be errors in the execution of transactions, delays in their settling, and losses sustained from the default of counterparties. Fourth, there are risks arising from financial transactions of the investment manager itself. Operating expenditures incurred in running the business and financial positions taken by the firm on its own account create risks of insolvency.

1.4   Fraud and problems in the investment management process create direct liabilities to clients. The costs of financial collapse of an investment manager are more indirect, and are limited to inconvenience and disruption, provided that clients' assets and monies are separated from those of the firm. If they are not, then clients' assets and monies may be at risk.

1.5 This chapter is concerned with the risks described in paragraph 1.3 and their effects on investors. While portfolio performance has been the subject of extensive analysis, as far as we are aware there has been no serious analysis of the other classes of risk. The approach taken here has been to combine analysis of published data with interviews and surveys.

1.6 The chapter draws heavily on the results of a series of interviews that were undertaken with investment managers over the period January–June 1988. A sample of 22 firms in the investment management business was selected on the basis of their activities, size, and location. Five of the sample were unit trusts, two were pension funds, two were trustees, and 13 performed a combination of unit trust, pension, and private client business. The purpose of the interviews was to establish first the frequency and scale of different classes of risk, and second the respective liability of investor and firm to losses sustained. To address these issues two questionnaires were designed, one for unit trust managers and one for other investment managers. The difference between the two reflected the greater relevance of own-positions (held in the 'box') to unit trust managers.

1.7 After the interviews had been completed, a questionnaire was sent to 100 members of IMRO in July 1988. The purpose of the survey was to make more precise the impressions gained from the interviews. In particular, quantitative information on risks was sought. As Chapter 7 describes, the implementation of appropriate capital requirements presupposes a precise description of the risks borne, the correlation between different types of risk, and the incidence of losses between investor and firm. A survey was the only way in which such detailed information could be assembled in a systematic fashion. Appendix I reproduces this survey.

1.8 The 100 firms were randomly selected by IMRO. Replies were received from 40 firms. Of these, 32 provided information that has been used in this analysis; the remaining eight did not provide precise or quantifiable information. Three of the respondents were unit trusts, two pension funds, and three private clients' businesses. The remaining 24 performed a range of activities. In the light of the sample size, the results of the survey can only be impressionistic, but we believe that they provide valuable support for the evidence given in interviews.

1.9 This chapter reports the results of the interviews and survey. Section 2 discusses the risks arising from the investment management process: execution errors, settlement delays, and counterparty default. Section 3 describes the financial risks arising from operating an investment management business and taking positions on own account. It describes the extent to which an investor is likely to be affected by insolvency of an IM firm. These two sections draw heavily on the interviews and survey. More direct evidence on financial risks is available from examining market data on investment management; this is reported in Section 4. Section 5 compares IMRO's capital requirements for individual firms with actual capital held, and Section 6 summarizes the results of the chapter.

SECTION 2 Risks Arising from the Investment Management Process

2.1 The previous chapter distinguished between investment advisers and managers. Firms that act in a purely advisory capacity do not execute transactions on behalf of clients. This section of the chapter therefore applies only to firms that manage clients' portfolios. Part A examines execution errors, Part B settlement risk, and Part C counterparty risk.

Part A Execution Errors

2.2 Execution errors may arise at one of four points. First, errors may be made in the interpretation of instructions received from clients. Second, there may be internal errors in the transmission of instructions from the investment manager. Third, errors may be made in communicating instructions to third parties such as brokers, market-makers, and custodian banks. Finally, errors may be made by the third party.

2.3 Common types of execution errors include those arising from (a) an incorrect amount of stock being bought or sold by an IM company, (b) a sale intended as a purchase (or vice versa), or (c) delays in executing instructions from a client by an IM company or its brokers. Such errors may be the result of negligence, or genuine misunderstandings.

2.4 Since many instructions are issued over the telephone, it may be difficult to distinguish negligence from misunderstandings or even from false claims of execution errors. Particular problems have been encountered by some firms managing private clients' accounts. In the aftermath of the October 1987 crash, some unit trust managers experienced a spate of claims of execution errors by clients; for example, there were incidences of clients claiming that sale instead of purchase orders had been placed. One unit trust management firm spoke of potential losses of £0.5 million arising from such disputed errors. The recording of telephone orders resolved many of those misunderstandings, and 75 per cent of the possible loss was recovered.

2.5 Nine out of the 32 firms in the survey reported that compensation was paid to clients during the six-month period. They were asked to report the 'largest' sum paid to an individual client. The amounts ranged from £6,950 to £86,000 with a mean value of £39,273.

2.6 The aggregate number of complaints received by each firm was also investigated for the same six-month period. The majority of firms reported no complaints (61.1 per cent), or stated that the figures were not available (11.1 per cent). One firm reported 41 complaints. The amounts in dispute among those firms reporting complaints ranged from £5,000 to £350,000. For the largest, the number of complaints totalled in excess of 26.

2.7 The number and size of execution errors can be influenced by many factors, including the administrative efficiency of the IM firm, the time it takes to monitor and reverse errors, the volatility of markets, and the volatility of particular securities caused by such events as merger announcements. In addition, our interviews suggest that the type of transaction is important: the frequency of errors was described as being lower in (a) gilt than equity transactions, (b) domestic than overseas securities, and (c) discretionary than non-discretionary portfolios. These impressions were confirmed by the survey. Three respondents reported execution errors in bond markets over the period October 1987– March 1988, while five reported them in equity markets. More errors were encountered in overseas than in domestic markets, though in some cases the sizes of execution errors were greater in domestic markets. Large errors tend to arise in overseas markets because of maladministration in foreign institutions, language difficulties, time differences that prevent early correction of errors, and a lack of familiarity with overseas practice. The factors influencing execution errors are summarized in Figure 3.1.

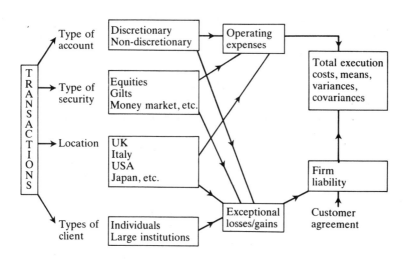

Fig. 3.1 The risks I: execution errors

2.8   One IM firm claimed that execution errors arose when IM functions such as custodianship were subcontracted. This suggests that investment management risks are not necessarily eliminated by subcontracting activities. The volume of execution errors varies enormously across firms and over time. One firm spoke of '30 per cent of contracts being re-booked at one time, although the figure was now down to 3 or 4 per cent'. Other comments included '5–10 per cent of deals create small problems', and '3–5 per cent of deals are re-booked but the vast majority are corrected on the same dealing day'.

2.9   The aggregate value of execution errors for an individual firm can be very uncertain. Most firms interviewed did not make a specific provision for execution errors, in the belief that in aggregate they could be positive or negative and the expected value was zero. However, there were exceptions, with one firm reporting 'a net loss of £0.5 million in errors and disagreements for 1987'. Another small firm reported a loss of £0.44 million from selling too much stock prior to a merger.

2.10   The survey presents a similar picture. Only nine of the 32 respondents to the survey reported significant execution errors, but in five cases errors amounted to 30 per cent of the value of their transactions over the six months from October 1987 to March 1988. One firm reported loses of £0.65 million arising from execution errors over the six months; another reported £0.13 million. Similarly, only four of the 21 unit trusts in the survey reported errors in the pricing of units, but in two cases errors remained uncorrected for four months and in one case they related to £4.1 million worth of units. The largest adjustment to prices that had to be made was 3 per cent.

2.11   Respondents to the survey described the actual or potential losses that could occur in relation to the size of the capital requirements imposed by IMRO. Questions on losses related to the following: (a) losses arising from errors in transactions conducted between October 1987 and March 1988, (b) the largest amount that firms paid to a client for losses incurred, and (c) losses incurred owing to errors in pricing units (of unit trusts). In each of these cases, the mean of the losses incurred expressed as a percentage of the individual firm's capital requirements was less than 6 per cent, indicating that the capital requirement set was far in excess of losses incurred. For amounts in dispute (i.e. potential losses), the percentage was 4.6 per cent.

2.12 Execution errors create two types of costs: an administrative cost arising from monitoring and reversing errors, and the loss (or gain) realized from price changes. As Figure 3.1 illustrates, the former is frequently regarded as part of the operating costs of running an IM business. For the six-month period, the average number of man-days spent on correcting execution errors and settlement days was recorded as being 40 by respondents to the survey. The largest number of man-days was 150 and the smallest zero. The average administrative cost was £16,600 with the largest recorded being £75,000

2.13 Administrative costs are borne by the IM firm. But individual errors may be for the account of the investor, the IM firm, or one of its agents. The incidence of loss depends on whether negligence is involved and can be proven, and upon the contractual relationship between the parties. Such relationships may be both formal and informal. One IM firm allowed its overseas broker to retain large gains from an execution error on the understanding that they would bear any costs from future errors.

2.14 Serious differences in view were expressed among those interviewed about clients' liability for execution errors. Some IM firms denied any liability unless they were negligent. In such a case the IM firm would make 'best efforts' to recover losses from negligent agents, but in the last resort unrecovered losses were for the client's account. Another firm believed all errors were for its own account even if other parties were negligent and refused to compensate for losses. Differences of opinion sometimes gave way to confusion. For example, one unit trust manager claimed that, if a trustee accepted shares that were incorrectly purchased, the error would have to be absorbed by the trustee's account. A trustee took a different view and said that he would expect the IM firm to make up any loss. The responses to the survey support the view that losses are for the firm's account. In all cases where losses were recorded they were borne by the firm; no losses had been incurred by clients.

2.15 Greater clarification is clearly required of liability for losses. This could be achieved by making contractual relations between IM firms and their clients more explicit or requiring statements of 'best practice' by the industry.

2.16 It is interesting to note that *no* respondent to the survey provided capital to meet execution errors. However, 27 of the 32 respondents had indemnity insurance amounting to an average £14.1 million, with an average excess of £0.7 million.

2.17 To summarize:
(a) It is not uncommon for firms to encounter execution errors. For the most part they are small and readily corrected. This is regarded by many firms as a normal part of their business, and the administrative costs arising (ranging between zero and £75,000) are part of a firm's overall operating costs.

(b) Large execution errors are very infrequent for an individual firm. However, when they occur they can represent a significant fraction of the total value of business done by a firm. Most firms protected themselves against large losses through indemnity insurance policies.

Part B   Settlement Risk

2.18 Settlement delays arise when, for example, one IM firm sells stock and fails to settle because it is unable to deliver stock certificates. Lack of delivery may arise because certificates have been lost or mislaid by the custodian, or because certificates were not delivered to the IM firm when the original purchase was made, or because of delays by registrars in issuing certificates. Delivery may not have taken place because of 'back-office problems' in the particular broker, or because frequency of sales of a particular stock created a chain of delays. In this case, the failure to settle results in a delay in the receipt of monies and an interest loss. Alternatively, for purchases of stock, a failure to settle creates an interest gain.

2.19 Over the past few years, settlement delays have been extensive. They have been greater in equity markets than gilts since the government is efficient at maintaining a register of ownership and retains certificates. Only four respondents to the survey reported settlement delays in bond markets, while nine firms reported them in equity markets. Problems have been more severe in dealings with some brokers than with others, and in particular with brokers in overseas equity markets, especially those of Spain and Italy. However, delays have been encountered in France, Portugal and even the USA. Problems have been few in Eurobond markets where settlement is made through Euroclear.

2.20 The extent and cost of settlement delays is illustrated by comments made in interviews: 'in Italy people were out of the money for eighteen months; as a result we required a line of credit totalling £16 million'; '£20 million in financing was required for one transaction where settlement was two weeks late'. Another firm 'allowed £10 million in capital to finance settlement delays'; while another required a £60 million line of credit for 1987. One firm talked of unmatched bargains going back a year, while another spoke of '10–15 per cent of deals subject to settlement delays'.

2.21 The survey paints a similar picture. Six cases of losses arising from settlement delays were cited with the largest being £150,000. One firm quoted £10 million as the amount of finance (bank borrowing or reserves) required to meet settlement delays, another reported £5–10 million, and a third £3 million. Eight firms cited cases of transactions negotiated during the last quarter of 1987 that remained unsettled at the end of the first quarter of 1988, but in all cases the value of transactions involved was less than 1 per cent of the total value of transactions negotiated over that period. Thus, while the amount of finance that may be required to cover a settlement delay can be substantial, large losses are rare. Furthermore, since the period over which settlement can be delayed is closely related to the level of activity in a market, costs tend to be concentrated at times when fee and commission income may be high. The solvency of IM firms is not therefore as a rule threatened by settlement delays. The exposure of investors to this class of risk will be further diminished in the UK when a depository system is introduced as part of the automation of the London Stock Exchange settlement process.

[handwritten margin note: This risk doesn't exist if this has now happened]

2.22 The interest costs of settlement delays may be borne by the original client, the IM company, or the broker. A substantial proportion interviewed settled with clients regardless of when monies were actually received. Thus, delays may involve interest costs or gains to the IM company depending upon whether it is a net seller or net buyer of stock. One firm in the survey reported a loss of £150,000, another a gain of £200,000. A minority of those interviewed regarded settlement delays as being for the client's account. Two cases were cited in the survey in which clients had borne losses of £10,000 as a consequence of settlement delays. Such differences in policy could not be explained by distinctions between discretionary and non-discretionary transactions. If client orders were combined, there seemed to be more likelihood of settlement being borne by the IM company. Similarly, if the broker was part of the same firm, settlement costs were more likely to be charged to the IM company's account. Figure 3.2 describes the causes and costs of settlement delays.

2.23 The losses or costs experienced by firms as a result of settlement delays may be expressed as a percentage of the individual firms' capital requirements. The costs of correcting execution errors and settlement delays were on average less than 3 per cent of a firm's capital requirements (six respondents). The largest loss actually incurred as a consequence of settlement delays was 4.5 per cent.

2.24 Unsettled transactions represent a potential risk to the firm. In eight cases, the total value of unsettled transactions for each

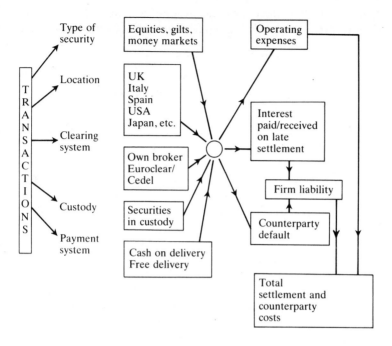

Fig. 3.2 The risks II: settlement delays and counterparty defaults

firm, if expressed as a proportion of the average firm's capital requirement, was 39.1 per cent. Only in one case was the maximum amount outstanding greater than the firm's capital requirements. The implication is that settlement risk on its own is not a threat to the solvency of most IM firms.

Part C Counterparty Risk

2.25 The risk of a delay in settlement should be compared with a risk of a default. Counterparty default arises when a broker, dealer, or bank fails to settle at all as a consequence of financial insolvency.

2.26 Very few companies have encountered counterparty default. One firm that was interviewed claimed they had experienced 'one default in ten years'. Another lost substantial amounts as a result of Hedderwick's failure, but losses were repaid from the Stock Exchange Compensation Fund. Two cases of default were cited by respondents to the survey, one in 1963 involving $1 million of foreign exchange, and one in 1983 involving £10,000 worth of UK gilts.

2.27 Even so, many firms admitted that they had been concerned about their counterparties during the 1987 crash, and some firms stated that they were reviewing the list of parties with whom they dealt. Comments included 'we stopped dealing with one currency dealer'; 'quite concerned about one relatively large broker'; 'reviewed counterparties around crash and changed many names, especially those abroad'; and 'suspected two US firms were in trouble and suspended dealings with them'. One large firm claimed they had not reviewed their counterparties at all but would do so in the light of the interview. Another said that they 'were not worried about counterparty risk since the Stock Exchange Fund stood behind the transaction'. These comments suggested either that counterparty risk is borne by IM firms or that firms felt obligated to protect their clients against such risks.

2.28 The survey asked firms how much they could have lost if (a) one of their counterparties had defaulted on 31 March 1988 and (b) all their counterparties had defaulted on that date. The average amount recorded by those firms responding to this question was £3.9 million for a single default by their largest counterparty and £35 million if all their counterparties had defaulted.

2.29 Expressed as a percentage of capital requirements, potential losses from counterparty risk exceeded 100 per cent on average. For the sample of firms, if one counterparty defaulted the loss would be on average 4.96 times the capital requirement; if all counterparties defaulted, it would be 28.47 times for the same sample. This illustrates the importance of counterparty risk and its potential impact on the solvency of IM firms.

2.30 While the nature of costs arising from counterparty default is clear, there was a wide disparity in view about how liability was allocated between investor and firm. In principle, a distinction can be drawn between a discretionary agent and principal. The latter initiates transactions and therefore bears the risk of failure; the former is merely acting on behalf of investors and does not bear settlement risk, except where negligence can be demonstrated.

2.31 In practice, liability is far more opaque. Some firms pointed to contract notes as evidence that losses were unequivocally for clients' accounts. Others claimed that losses must be borne by IM firms since either advice (rather than contract) notes were sent to clients and clients were unaware of the names of brokers, or IM firms were responsible for choosing brokers. Most managers thought that clients expected them to bear the cost of counterparty default and felt that their reputation would be adversely affected if they failed to do so.

2.32 The divergent views about liability for counterparty default are reflected in responses to the survey. In the two cases of actual counterparty default cited by respondents, counterparty loss was borne by the firm. However, in the event of counterparty default occurring in the future, only four thought that their firm would bear the loss while eight thought that clients would. There is considerable uncertainty in the investment management business about how liability for counterparty default is distributed between investor and firm.

2.33 It is interesting to note that no firm in the survey had made provision for counterparty default.

SECTION 3   Financial Risks: Evidence from Interviews and the Survey

3.1   The value of an IM business can be divided into an intangible and a tangible component. The intangible value relates to the capitalized value of future fee income. The tangible value relates to the value of fixed assets, and the firm's own portfolio of securities. This division of values may be important in assessing the risks of the IM business.

3.2   Financial failure affects the investor in two ways. First, there is disruption arising from the freezing of assets and monies during insolvency proceedings, and inconvenience from having to transfer investments to new management once they are unfrozen. Second, and more seriously, if clients' monies have not been clearly and properly segregated from those of the firm, then all creditors may have a claim against clients' monies in an insolvency.

3.3   This section examines the risks and costs of financial failure. Part A examines the risks associated with management activities (intangible assets); Part B considers fixed assets and own positions (tangible assets); and Part C discusses the costs to investors of financial failure.

Part A   Management Activities

3.4   The risk to intangible values is affected by the volatility of fee income and the size of operating costs. Fee income is in part determined by the level of market prices, since, as discussed in the previous chapter, fees are directly or indirectly related to the market values of securities and the size of portfolios under management. Figure 3.3 illustrates how volatile net flows into the unit trust business have been.

3.5   Volatile fee income creates risks if some of the costs of running an IM business are fixed. Costs may be fixed in the long run—minimum levels of expenditure to run an IM business—or

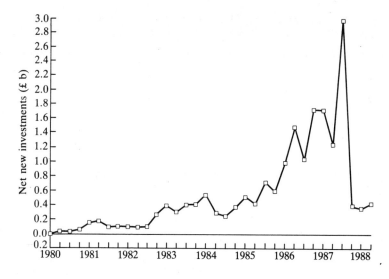

Fig. 3.3 Net new investments in unit trusts, 1980–1988
Source: Unit Trust Association

variable in the long run but fixed in the short term—costs of adjusting to lower levels of expenditure.

3.6 It is not easy to measure the proportion of fixed costs in the IM business. In large part, it is dependent on the extent to which salaries can be reduced without impairing the efficiency of the business. One party interviewed stated that directors would take large reductions in pay before redundancies were declared. Other firms argued that salaries could not be radically reduced without undermining the quality of personnel employed and services provided.

3.7 The survey indicates the extent to which costs are fixed. Respondents to the survey cited £6 million as being on average the minimum expenditure required to run the business. Four firms recorded levels in excess of £10 million. The lowest figure quoted was £10,000.

3.8 In addition, disruption may be caused by attempts to reduce expenditure rapidly in response to financial problems. An important consideration that arises in this regard is whether variations in fee income are idiosyncratic or are closely correlated across firms. It may be difficult for individual firms to absorb reductions in their earnings that are not mirrored in other firms.

Part B   Fixed Assets and Own Positions

3.9   The assets of the IM business may be financed with equity or debt. If debt is used, then the total gearing of the firm includes capital as well as operating gearing.

3.10   Some IM firms take positions. These can arise from underwriting (or sub-underwriting), long or short positions in individual securities, and the market-making function of the unit trust 'box'. Own positions may be especially risky. For example, underwriting is like selling (i.e writing) a put option to companies issuing shares. The volatility of those options may be much higher than that of the underlying equity.

3.11   Seven of the firms involved in the survey gave details of investments made on their own accounts at the end of December 1987 and at the end of March 1988. Own investments ranged from £3,000 to almost £14 million. Four firms held equities, with two investing in both domestic and foreign securities.

3.12   Three firms reported that they wrote options over the six months October 1987–March 1988. One firm had written £25.5 million of options; the other two had written £0.5 million and £1 million respectively. Three firms had underwritten securities. The largest value of securities underwritten was £7.5 million; the other two were around £4 million.

3.13   Unit trust managers that take positions in units (referred to as the 'box') essentially act as market-makers. 'Boxes' tend to make money when markets are rising and the 'box' is long in securities. They are less likely to make money in falling markets, since managers are not allowed to take short positions.

3.14 Eight firms reported running 'boxes' over the six months October 1987–March 1988. They reported the average size of their 'box' and its maximum value for the period covered. Three firms explicitly stated that they did not run 'boxes'. Of those that did, the average size of the 'box' over the period was £1.5 million and the average of the maximum size of 'box' reported was £3.9 million. The largest recorded was £11.7 million.

3.15 New rules about the pricing of units have been introduced. These will encourage firms to price units on a forward basis when they are created and redeemed rather than on a historic (backward) basis. Five respondents to the survey indicated that they intended to move on to a forward basis, three that they would retain the historic pricing basis, and two that they would use a mixture of the two (depending on the time of day).

3.16 Six of the eight unit trusts (UTs) taking positions said that they provide (or should provide) capital to cover risks. The average amount recorded was £370,000; one firm reported £2 million. One firm said that it held (or should hold) capital to cover its positions. In sharp contrast to execution errors and counterparty risk, therefore, firms in our sample that take positions, either in the 'box' or in some other form, hold capital.

Part C   The Costs to Investors of Financial Failure

3.17 If clients' balances are not separated, as may be the case with IM firms that are also banks or part of a banking group, a loss may arise if the group defaults. In that case, the investor may simply become a creditor of the firm in receivership or liquidation. Even if clients' balances are formally separated, interviews with IM firms suggest that investors' money may be at risk for short periods of time between receipt and deposit into a client's account.

3.18 No firm in the survey held clients' monies on its own account for an appreciable length of time at 30 June 1988.

However, three firms acknowledged holding clients' money temporarily on the firm's account. Usually this was for less than a day, but one firm reported that it could be for up to ten days. Furthermore, eight firms held dividend and interest receipts on their own accounts before transferring them to clients' accounts. In most cases this was completed in one to two days, but one firm said it could take up to one-and-a-half months.

3.19   Unit trusts provide an example of where client funds are not immediately credited to a client's account. If an investor's funds are received by a unit trust at the beginning of a day but units are not credited until the end of the day, and if the IM firm defaulted during the day, then the client could become a general creditor of the firm.

3.20   Most firms (13 respondents to the survey) register clients' securities in clients' names. However, a significant number also register securities in the firm's name on behalf of clients. Seven respondents to the survey reported doing this at the end of March 1988. In one case the amount registered in the firm's name was £87 million, and the average recorded was £15 million.

3.21   If clients' monies and assets are clearly separated from those of the firm, the potential loss to the investor arising from financial failure is restricted to disruption, inconvenience, and fraud. Cash balances may be frozen leading to a loss of liquidity. Portfolios may be frozen with a loss of management supervision and a deterioration in performance.

3.22   In the subsequent analysis, client balances will be analysed as if they were not separated from the IM firm's bank accounts. As a result, if the IM firm defaulted, it will be assumed that client funds could be used to meet the general expenses of the firm. Should the firm default, clients would become general creditors of the firm.

3.23 A numerical example will be used to illustrate how the value of clients' funds can be eroded by default in the absence of separation. The possibility of fraud is not entertained.

3.24 Consider a firm that does separate clients' monies and assets. Suppose that the firm has assets with a value of £100 million and loans outstanding of £30 million, and that the annual volatility of the firm's assets is 40 per cent (somewhat higher than the average volatility of the UK equity market). If the firm becomes insolvent, then the only cost that investors suffer is a disruption cost. Suppose this cost takes the form of investors earning a return of 10 per cent less than they would do if their assets were not frozen. Finally, assume that the IM firm is monitored every three months. Under these assumptions, the *expected* cost of disruption to the investor is just 0.8 pence per pound of assets invested. The shorter (longer) the period of monitoring, the lower (higher) the expected costs of disruption. These disruption costs appear relatively low.

3.25 Now assume that the IM company does not separate client balances, and that in the event of default the client becomes a creditor of the firm. In this case, any probability of default by the IM firm will reduce the value of client balances. Suppose that the value of the IM firm's assets is £100 million, as before, and the volatility of assets is again 40 per cent. The book value of the debt is now taken to be £38 million. In addition, we assume the rate of interest on short-term government bonds is 10 per cent and, for simplicity only, that no dividends are paid by the company to its shareholders.

3.26 Losses to investors will be calculated for four sizes of clients' balances: £10 million, £100 million, £200 million, and £1,000 million. In the event of default they rank equally with the other debts of IM firms. Using an option pricing model to value the risky debt, the risk premium required to compensate client balances for default risk has been estimated. The size of the losses ranges from 0 pence for each pound of client's balances in the case of £10

million of clients' funds to 9.19 pence for each pound of client
balances with £1,000 million of clients' funds.

Amount of clients' money (£m)	Expected losses to clients' money (pence in the pound)
10	0
100	3.76
200	5.88
1000	9.19

Costs to investors of financial failure are therefore highly
dependent on the value of client balances held on the firm's
account.

3.27 The size of loss will also depend significantly on the period
of monitoring. In the previous example, the monitoring period was
one year. If the period were contracted to three months, the loss to
investors would range from 0 to 2.18 pence in the pound. Were the
monitoring period increased to two years, the losses would range
from 0.36 to 13.34 pence in the pound.

3.28 This analysis suggests that disruption costs may be relatively
small, but that losses to investors from non-separation of client
balances (excluding fraud) may be significant.

SECTION 4　Financial Risks: Evidence from Share Price Data

4.1 In this section we describe the results of simulations that
suggest that IM firms' assets and equities are of above-average
risk. Using data from a sample of traded IM firms, the measured
risk of equities is shown. The purpose is to provide some
impression of how an IM firm's income and assets would be eroded
in the event of a fall in the prices of market securities.

4.2 Table 3.1 records the equity risk of pure IM firms traded on
the London Stock Exchange. Equity risk is captured by the beta
coefficient, which measures the sensitivity of a stock's returns to
changes in a market index. (The latter is a proxy for economy-wide

Table 3.1 Equity risks of quoted investment management companies, 1988

	Beta* (1)	Standard deviation:* stock prices (%) (2)	Implied standard deviation: options data (3)	Debt / Debt+equity Book values† (%) (4)	Debt / Debt+equity Market values (%) (5)
Berkeley Govett			45	0.00	0.00
Britannia Arrow Holdings	1.46	47	39	28.88	12.51
Edinburgh Fund Managers	1.03	43	44	21.50	4.65
Framlington	0.98	39	43	30.64	7.89
G.T. Management	1.32	54	43	6.18	1.79
Henderson	1.58	44	45	0.00	0.00
Ivory & Syme	1.29	46		0.00	0.00
M & G	1.05	41	42	0.00	0.00
Mercury Asset Management	1.49	70	42	20.17	0.59
Perpetual	1.14	60	40	11.70	0.98
Templeton			40	38.51	
Market	1.00	30			

* The beta coefficients and standard deviations in columns (1) and (2) are based on five years of data to end-March 1988.
† Gearing estimates do not reflect client balances held by the firm.

risks). A beta coefficient greater than unity means that the riskiness of a firm is greater than that of the market index. The index can be thought of as representing the average firm in the economy. Except in two cases, the estimated betas are taken from the London Business School's Risk Measurement Service. Little attention should be paid to figures for individual firms. However, in all cases estimates are 1 or above, suggesting that IM firms are of above-average risk.

4.3 An alternative measure is the volatility or standard deviation of the return on a company's equity. This captures both economy-wide risks (measured by beta) and those risks unique to the firm. The standard deviations are calculated from two sources of data, stock prices and options data. In both cases, estimates are substantially above 30 per cent—the average standard deviation of quoted companies. Again, pure IM companies are of above-average risk.

4.4 One reason for IM companies being of above-average risk might be that they are unusually highly capital-geared. But Table 3.1 records the fact that IM companies display unusually *low* levels of gearing. Risk cannot therefore be attributed to finance; rather, it must be due to the underlying assets.

4.5 Were all the costs of running an investment management business variable, then volatile fee income would not create a solvency risk. But, as described in Section 3, some operating costs are not entirely variable, and as a consequence they create a risk similar to that associated with financial gearing. The way in which operational and financial risk affect the overall riskiness of a firm is described in a simple example in Appendix II. In the case cited in Appendix II, an ungeared firm with fixed costs of one-third aggregate costs has a beta coefficient 40 per cent above the average, even though the funds under management are indexed funds and, therefore, only of average risk, i.e. unit beta. Fixed costs introduce an additional level of operating gearing between revenues and profits. This may help to explain an observation in the *Financial Times* (February 1989) which states: 'Their [investment management] fixed costs operations are highly geared to the level of the market, with higher share prices flowing directly into fatter fees; Kitcat and Aitken, for example, estimates that a 20 per cent rise in the market could boost the earnings of Henderson Administration and GT Management by 80 per cent.'

4.6 The survey sought information about the costs of running the business for the periods April 1987–September 1987 and October 1987–March 1988. Of the 31 firms that gave quantitative answers, 14 reported a deficit of expenditure over receipts in at least one of the periods studied. The average value of cash receipts minus cash expenditures for the two periods was £837,683 and £320,687, respectively. The range for the April–September period was − £7,958,000 to £10,200,000. For the October–March period the range was −£5,748,498 to £2,673,000.

4.7 Firms were also asked to quantify their minimum level of expenditures. Twenty-eight out of 36 firms gave quantitative replies. The average minimum level was £5,765,000 but the spread was, as expected, very large. The range, expressed as a proportion of the firm's capital requirements, was from 12.7 to 1661.9 per cent with an average of 658 per cent.

4.8 To evaluate the usefulness of beta as a measure of an equity's risk (or volatility), the share price performance of the IM quoted firms in the immediate aftermath of the stock market crash has been compared with movements in an index (the FTSE index) of London share prices. In Table 3.2, it is shown that the market declined over the six-week period by 32 per cent (from an index level of 100 to 68.0). An equally weighted index of IM companies listed in Table 3.1 declined by 52 per cent. The above-average decline is consistent with the above-average measures of risk recorded in Table 3.1.

4.9 Table 3.3 ranks the ten IM firms by the size of their share price decline between 14 October and 30 November 1987. It also lists their beta coefficients. Visual inspection suggests that the greater the price fall from the October crash period (i.e. the smaller the level of the index), the greater is the estimated beta coefficient. This implies that firms with higher betas have higher equity volatilities as predicted by the definition of these risk measures.

Table 3.2 Index of share price movements of 10 quoted IM companies around the time of the 1987 crash (14 Oct. 1987 = 100)

	14 Oct.	19 Oct.	20 Oct.	21 Oct.	22 Oct.	23 Oct.	26 Oct.	2 Nov.	9 Nov.	16 Nov.	23 Nov.	30 Nov.
Ave. of IM companies*	100	92.7	78.7	82.1	79.7	76.7	66.0	64.6	66.3	62.7	60.1	47.6
FTSE	100	88.4	77.6	83.7	78.9	76.4	72.5	74.2	67.4	72.5	71.4	68.0

* In two cases IM firms are part of a larger group (Britannia Arrow and Berkeley & Govett).

Table 3.3 Beta coefficients explain much of the cross-sectional variations in share price falls around the 1987 stock market crash

Company	Price index on 30 Nov. 1987 (14 Oct. 1987 = 100)	Beta coefficient
Berkeley Govett	64.6	—
Edinburgh Fund Management	57.1	1.03
Perpetual	52.5	1.14
Ivory & Syme	51.0	1.29
M & G	45.2	1.05
Templeton	44.5	—
G.T. Management	42.3	1.32
Mercury Asset Management	42.2	1.49
Britannia Arrow Holdings	41.9	1.46
Henderson	34.7	1.58

4.10   However, the IM firms listed may not be representative of the industry as a whole. They are for example less diversified than IM businesses held by diversified financial groups. In the case of the Prudential, its beta coefficient is 0.92 (i.e. below-average risk) and its volatility (standard deviation) is 26 per cent annually, below the market average of 30 per cent. We suspect that diversified financial groups have similar risks to the Prudential.

SUMMARY 5   Summary of Chapter 3

5.1   This chapter has described two classes of risk that investors face when employing firms to manage or advise on the management of their portfolios.

5.2   The first class, risks associated with the investment management process, comprised execution errors, settlement delays, and counterparty default. Losses on these accounts may establish direct liabilities of investment managers to their clients. In fact, in many cases there was considerable uncertainty as to how such costs would be distributed between investor and firm. Execution errors are most likely to establish corporate liabilities. But even here, except where negligence can be demonstrated, investment managers differed in the liability that they accepted. In relation to settlement and counterparty risk, in theory, a distinction can be drawn between discretionary agents and principals. In practice, the distinction appears much more opaque, with some firms regarding their responsibility as falling well short of full compensation for counterparty failures.

5.3   Execution errors created two classes of costs for IM firms: administrative expenses, and liabilities to investors. Small execution errors were not uncommon. Large losses were rare, but when they did occur they could impose substantial burdens on firms.

5.4   Several cases were cited of delays in settlement that had created a need for temporary access to substantial amounts of capital. This could come from reserves or from loan facilities. However, settlement delays on their own are unlikely to jeopardize the financial solvency of a firm. They can be to the benefit as well as to the cost of IM firms, and tend to be concentrated in prosperous periods of buoyant activity.

5.5   Counterparty default was even more exceptional than large losses arising from execution errors and settlement delays. If counterparty default did occur, then IM firms could be faced with devastating losses, particularly if default afflicted more than one counterparty. Chapter 6 will discuss ways of protecting investors against these kinds of risks.

5.6   Some IM firms were not always clear as to who should bear the losses arising from counterparty risk. It is reasonable to assume that some clients are even less certain about liabilities.

5.7   The second class of risks—financial risks—resulted from the operation of an investment manager, investment in fixed assets, and own positions. Even if a firm held no fixed assets and took no positions, financial distress could result from the fixed nature of its expenditures, in particular salaries. It is difficult to establish the extent to which costs are fixed or inflexible, but responses to the survey suggest that minimum expenditures to run the business are appreciable. Furthermore, investment managers were found to have beta coefficients and standard deviations of returns that were significantly above average. This is confirmed by an examination of movements in share prices of investment managers around the time of the crash. Since the financial gearing levels of investment managers are in general small, this suggests that the fixed component of operating costs is not insignificant.

5.8 In the past, unit trust managers have had substantial own positions in the 'box'. Changes in pricing practice are likely to alter this. Other cases of firms taking positions on their own account were noted.

5.9 Financial failures impose two types of costs on investors: disruption costs, where clients' monies have been separated, and dilution of investors' claims in the event of insolvency, where they have not. The latter is potentially much more serious than the former and argues strongly for the separation of clients' balances. Even where separation is in principle practised, investors could suffer losses from the temporary holding of clients' monies in company accounts.

A Survey of Investment Managers

Introduction

This questionnaire relates to those activities of your firm that have been registered with the Investment Management Regulatory Organization (IMRO). It refers to the six months from October 1987 to March 1988.

The questionnaire is in seven parts. Part A seeks information relating to the transactions that you undertake for clients or on your own account. It requests details of errors that you have encountered in transacting with dealers and brokers and disputes that have arisen with clients. Part B refers to delays in the settlement of transactions. Part C relates to risks of your counterparties defaulting on their obligations. Part D examines positions that you take (if any) on your own account. Part E considers the fixed costs of running your business. Part F asks about the handling of clients' money. Finally, part G requests information about the costs of complying with regulatory requirements.

All of the above are factors that are thought to influence the appropriate level of capitalization of member-firms.

Background Information

Name of your firm _____

Name of person answering this questionnaire _____

Position held in firm _____

Types of activities performed by your firm: _____

	Percentage by assets under management	Percentage by fee income
Unit trusts		
Investment trusts		
Pension funds		
Insurance		
Charities		
Private clients		
Other (please specify)		

A: Efforts that have been Encountered in Executing Transactions

This part of the questionnaire relates to transactions that you undertake on behalf of clients or on your own account. Information is requested relating to any errors that you have encountered when transacting with dealers, brokers, or other investment managers. These errors might arise from transactions in wrong securities, wrong amounts, transactions at incorrect prices, failures to meet specifications regarding transactions due to various factors.

1 Please describe the transactions by total value and number that you have executed with brokers, dealers, or other investment managers over the past six months (from October 1987 to March 1988):

	Total value of transactions	Number
Domestic equities		
Foreign equities		
Bonds		
Money market instruments		
Options and futures		
Commodities		
Other (please specify)		

2　What percentage of the above transactions by number and value were subject to errors of any form whatsoever?

	Percentage by	
	Value	Number
Domestic equities	_____	_____
Foreign equities	_____	_____
Bonds	_____	_____
Money market instruments	_____	_____
Options and futures	_____	_____
Commodities	_____	_____
Other (please specify)	_____	_____

3　What were the profits of losses (if any) associated with the above execution errors borne by

(a) your firm?　_____

(b) your clients?　_____

4　What was the average amount of capital that you provided over the six months October 1987 to March 1988 to meet execution errors?　_____

5　What is the largest amount that you have ever paid in compensation to a client　_____

6　How many complaints of any form whatsoever have you received from clients over the past six months (from October 1987 to March 1988)? What was the total amount that was in dispute over these six months?

	No. of complaints	Amounts in dispute
Investment businesses	_____	_____
Other corporate businesses	_____	_____
Private customers	_____	_____
Pension funds	_____	_____

Charities   _____   _____

Others   _____   _____

7 (a) What is the value of your indemnity insurance? _____

    (b) What is the excess on this insurance? _____

8 Please list the occasions during the period 1 October 1987–31 March 1988 on which an error in the pricing of units was discovered. Please state the period over which prices remained incorrect, the value of units created or cancelled at incorrect prices, and the percentage adjustment made to prices on correction.

Date on which error was discovered	Period for which prices remained incorrect	Value of units created or cancelled during the period (use a '+' for creation and a '−' for cancellation)	Percentage adjustment to prices (use a '+' for upwards and a '−' for downwards)
_____	_____	_____	_____
_____	_____	_____	_____

B: Settlement Problems

This part relates to problems of settlement that you encountered over the six months October 1987–March 1988.

9 What proportion (by value and number) of the transactions described in question 4 were subject to delayed settlement?

| | Percentage by | |
	Value	Number
Domestic equities	_____	_____
Foreign equities	_____	_____
Bonds	_____	_____

Money market instruments   _____   _____

Options and futures   _____   _____

Commodities   _____   _____

Other   _____   _____

10   What was total profit or loss (if any) associated with the above settlement delays borne by

(a) your firm?_____

(b) your clients?   _____

11   How large were the transactions negotiated between 1 October 1987 and 31 December 1987 that remained unsettled at 31 March 1988? Please record sales and purchases separately and show as a proportion of transactions negotiated in the last quarter of 1987.

	Value	Proportion of transactions
Purchases	_____	_____
Sales	_____	_____

12   Please estimate the number of man-days and the operating costs incurred by your firm over the six months October 1987–March 1988 in correcting execution errors and settlement delays. _____

13   What was your average financial requirement (bank borrowing or reserves) over the six months October 1987–March 1988 to meet settlement delays? _____

14   What is the largest loss that you have incurred as a consequence of settlement delays? _____

C: Counterparty Default

This part of the questionnaire relates to defaults by counterparties (e.g. brokers and dealers) on transactions that you have undertaken with them.

15   Has a counterparty with whom you deal ever failed to settle? If so, please list the occasions on which counterparties with whom you deal have failed to settle and the amounts involved. Please also describe the type (or types) of security associated with the default using the classification listed in questions 1 and 2.

Date	Amount	Type of security
————	————	————————
————	————	————————
————	————	————————

16   How much of the loss was borne by you and how much by your client?

Date	Amount borne by client	by firm	Amounts unaccounted for (please provide details, e.g. amounts paid by compensation schemes)
———	————	————	—————————————————————————
———	————	————	—————————————————————————

17   Given the extent of unsettled transactions on 31 March 1988, what was the largest loss that you could have incurred on that day if

(a) one counterparty with whom you deal had failed to settle? __

(b) all the counterparties with whom you deal had simultaneously failed to settle? _____

18   If you encountered counterparty default in the future, what proportion of any resulting loss would you expect to be borne by

(a) your firm? _____

(b) your clients? _____

(c) other parties? (please specify) _____

19   How large are the financial provisions that you make or think that you should make for possible losses arising from counterparty defaults? ____ _____

D: Position Risk

This part of the questionnaire relates to positions taken by your firm on its own account. Questions 24–28 are relevant only to the managers of unit trusts.

20   Please list investments made by your firm on its own account in the following at end December 1987 and end March 1988.

	End December 1987	End March 1988
Domestic equities		
Foreign equities		
Bonds		
Money market instruments		
Options and futures		
Commodities		
Other (please specify)		

12   What was the total value of options written by your firm on its own account over the six months October 1987–March 1988?

22   What was the total value of securities underwritten by your firm on its own account over the six months October 1987–March 1988?

23   How much capital do you provide or do you think that you should provide to cover your own position risks?

24   What were the average and largest sizes of the 'box' that you ran during the period October 1987–March 1988 inclusive?

(a) Average size _____
(b) Largest size_____

25   What was the total value of units

(a) created during the six months October 1987–March 1988?   __
(b) cancelled during the six months October 1987–March 1988? _____

26   What was the composition of units on 30 September 1987, 31 October 1987, and 31 December 1987?

	30 Sept.	31 Oct.	31 Dec.
Domestic equities			
α stocks	_____	_____	_____
β stocks	_____	_____	_____
γ stocks	_____	_____	_____
Foreign equities			
Europe	_____	_____	_____
Far East	_____	_____	_____
USA	_____	_____	_____
Other	_____	_____	_____
Bonds	_____	_____	_____
Money market instruments	_____	_____	_____
Options and futures	_____	_____	_____
Commodities	_____	_____	_____
Other	_____	_____	_____

27   Do you intend to price units on a forward or a backward basis in the future? _____

28   How much capital do you provide or do you think that you should provide to cover risks associated with

(a) running the 'box'? _____
(b) the creation and cancellation of units? _____

E: Fixed Costs

This part of the questionnaire asks for information about the fixed costs of running your business.

29   How large were cash inflows and outflows during the two six-month periods April 1987–September 1987 inclusive and October 1987–March 1988 inclusive?

	Apr. 1987–Sept. 1987	Oct. 1987–Mar. 1988
Cash receipts	_____	_____
Cash expenditures	_____	_____

30   How much working capital did you require to finance your business over these two periods? How much came from bank borrowing and how much from reserves?

	Bank borrowing	Reserves	Other
(a) Apr. 1987–to Sept. 1987	_____	_____	_____
(b) Oct. 1987–Mar. 1988	_____	_____	_____

31   What is the minimum level of expenditure required to operate your business? _____

F: Clients' Money

This part requests information about the holding of clients' money.

32   How much clients' money was held on their own accounts, how much was temporarily held on the firm's account in the process of being transferred to clients' accounts, and how much was held on the firm's account on behalf of clients at close of business on *30 June 1988*?

(a) Held on clients' accounts _____
(b) Temporarily held on firm's account in the process of being transferred to clients' accounts _____
(c) Held on firm's account on behalf of clients _____

33   When monies are first received from clients, for how long on average (in hours or days) are they initially held on the firm's account before being transferred to the client's account? _____

34   For how long are dividend and interest receipts on average initially held on the firm's account before being transferred to clients' accounts? _____

35   What was the value of securities registered in clients' names and the firm's name on behalf of clients at close of business on *30 June 1988*?

(a) Clients' names _____

(b) Firm's name on behalf of clients _____

G: Costs of Compliance

This final part seeks information on the costs of compliance that your firm has incurred and expects to incur over the coming year.

36 How many people do you employ on compliance activities? (Please state as the number of full-time equivalents.) _____

37 In the absence of regulatory requirements, how many people would you normally have employed on similar management functions? _____

38 What were the expenditures that you incurred on compliance activities over the six months October 1987–March 1988? _____

39 How much do you anticipate spending on compliance activities over the next twelve months? _____

40 What are your capital requirements under IMRO rules? How are these requirements arrived at? _____

41 How much capital do you currently hold? _____

42 What is the cost to your firm of providing additional capital? _____

A Simple Model of Operational and Financial Risk

A1 The purpose of the following model is to illustrate why IM businesses that are concentrated mainly in equities may have above-average industry risk.

A2 Initially, fee income will be assumed to be directly proportional to market values of funds managed. Also, funds will be assumed to be invested in equities equivalent to an indexed portfolio. The income statement is:

Income from own-positions		1
Fee income		10
		11
Fixed costs	2	
Variable costs	4	6
Profit		5

And the balance sheet is:

	£m
Tangible assets (own positions)	10
Intangible assets	40
Total assets	50

The value of intangibles is obtained by assuming a price–earnings ratio of 10 for profit on income excluding that from own positions ($10 \times 4 = 40$) and the value of tangibles from assuming a price–earnings (PE) ratio of 10 on income from own positions $(10 \times 1 = 10)$.

A3 By definition, the risk, referred to as 'beta', of the market index is 1.0; therefore if the beta (revenues) depends upon the value of the market, it is also 1.0. Using the relation between the beta (assets) and the beta (revenues), assets, and fixed costs,

$$\text{Beta (company)} = \text{Beta (revenues)} \times \frac{\text{Value of assets} + \text{value of fixed costs}}{\text{Value of assets}}$$

$$= 1.0 \times \frac{50 + 20}{50}$$

$$= 1.4.$$

The value of fixed costs (20) is obtained by capitalizing annual fixed costs of 2, assuming a PE ratio of 10. If the beta (revenues) is 1.0, the beta of the company is 1.4. The result suggests that an IM firm whose income results from managing equity portfolios similar to an index bears a risk 40 per cent greater than the index.

A4 It is the presence of fixed costs that has increased the risk of the IM business to above that of the market (and therefore above that of the average firm).

A5 If debt financing is used, the risk of the beta (equity) will be even greater than this. Using the relation between the beta (equity) and the beta (company),

$$\text{Beta (equity)} = \text{Beta (company)} \times \frac{\text{Equity} + \text{Debt}}{\text{Equity}},$$

assuming the beta of debt is zero. Assuming D/E is 0.25,

$$\text{Beta (equity)} = 1.4 \times \frac{40 + 10}{40}$$

$$= 1.68.$$

The equity beta of 1.68 compares with the beta of the equity index of 1.0. Thus, the beta of the IM firm is 68 per cent greater than that of the average equity.

The formulas used in this appendix are derived and explained in Brealey and Myers (1988).

4 Past Cases of Failure in the Investment Management Business

SECTION 1 Introduction

1.1 This chapter discusses past cases of failure in the UK investment management industry. In particular, the chapter focuses on the 'secondary banking crisis' of the early 1970s and the period 1979–87 during which there were several financial failures.

1.2 Section 2 examines cases of wealth transfers. It distinguishes between employee fraud against companies (Part A), direct theft of client funds (Part B), irregular dealings which involve violation of either legal or ethical guidelines (Part C), and companies established with the intention of making large returns at the expense of clients (Part D). Part E discusses levels of prosecutions for fraud. Section 3 examines cases where financial distress in either the IM firm or elsewhere in the group puts investors' funds at risk. Seven cases of financial difficulties are outlined in detail in the Appendix to the chapter. Section 4 considers the implications of the chapter for investor protection.

1.3 Fraud Squad data shown in Table 4.1 breaks down 'financial fraud' into three categories for the years 1985–7: commodities, stocks and securities, and investment management fraud.

Table 4.1 Cases of financial fraud perpetrated in the London region

	Commodities	Stocks and securities	Investment management
1985	9	2	16
1986	4	7	35
1987	7	7	23

Source: Metropolitan and City Fraud Squad.

1.4 One difficulty in assessing the level of fraudulent activity in investment management is that information is available only on detected and publicized cases, typically those involving financial collapse. By definition, where fraud is successful, it is undetected and thus unquantifiable. Even detected fraud is often not reported by the parties involved since firms frequently prefer to take internal action without involving the authorities or the police.

1.5 As an indicator of the size of funds involved, the Metropolitan and City Fraud Squads estimated in 1987 that the total 'money at risk' to financial fraud in the London region was £1,169 million. While 'money at risk' includes money that could possibly have been stolen, as well as monies that are known to have been stolen, the estimate suggests the potential scale of the problem should investor safeguards prove to be inadequate.

1.6 However, one striking observation in this chapter is that the value of client funds reported as lost is small. Tables 4.2 and 4.3 report amounts at risk and lost during the two periods 1973–5 and 1979–87. Table 4.2 reports companies where client funds were at risk because of pure financial risk, without fraud or malpractice. The largest client losses during the period under review were limited to around £5 million, though this picture may have changed in the light of recent cases. A second notable feature was the tendency for instances of fraud and irregular dealing to be exposed only after financial difficulties had led to the collapse of the company involved. Financial distress within a firm, caused in some cases by losses on own-account trading or through poor investment decisions, often appeared to be the reason for the loss of client funds. Client funds tended to be lost where they were not separated from company bank accounts. However, even with separation, client funds were sometimes lost because management had control over client bank accounts. Finally, in cases of financial distress affecting other parts of the group, client losses in the absence of fraud in the IM company were small. In several instances during the secondary banking crisis, investment management arms of troubled groups were disposed of with little or no disruption cost to investors.

Table 4.2 Companies where investors' money has been at risk, 1973–1975

	Company	Business	Cause of problem	Amounts of clients' funds at risk (£m)	Amounts of funds lost (£m)
1973	Cedar Holdings	Financial group	Secondary banking crisis	9.5	0.0
1974	J. H. Vavasseur	Financial group	Secondary banking crisis	24.8	0.0
1974	Oceanic Unit Trust*	Unit trust management	Secondary banking crisis	13.2	0.0
1974	National Group of Unit Trusts*	Unit trust management	Secondary banking crisis	92.0	0.0
1974	Jessel Securities	Industrial/financial group	Insurance related problems	42.0	0.0
1974	Keyser Ullman	Financial group	Secondary banking crisis	1.8	0.0
1974	Dawnay Day	Financial group	Secondary banking crisis	47.5	0.0
1974	London Wall Group	Unit trust management	Operating problems	9.3	0.0
1974	Portfolio Fund Managers	Unit trust management	Operating problems	2.5	0.0
1974	Surinvest Fund Managers	Unit trust management	Operating problems	4.3	0.0
1975	First National Finance Corp.	Financial group	Secondary banking crisis	0.1	0.0
1975	Slater Walker	Financial group	Secondary banking crisis	295.0	0.0

* Owned by Triumph Investment Trust.

Table 4.3 Companies where investors' money has been at risk, 1979–1987

	Company	Business	Nature of problem/outcome	Amounts of funds lost* (£m)
1979	Arbuthnot Latham Securities	Investment management	'Open account' trading	0.00
1980	Langford Scott & Partners	Licensed dealer-inv. mgt.	False accounting	N/A
1981	Imperial Commodities	Commodity broker/inv. mgt.	Wound up by DTI	0.30
1981	Farrington Stead	Investment management	Own-account trading losses	0.05
1981	Norton Warburg	Investment management	Fraud against client funds	4.50
1981	M. L. Doxford	Commodity broker/inv. mgt.	Own-account trading losses	1.13
1981	Miller Carnegie	Commodity broker/inv. mgt.	Wound up by DTI	0.32
1983	Global Capital Growth	Commodity broker/inv. mgt.	Dissolved	0.40
1984	Cornhill Securities	Commodity broker/inv. mgt.	Dissolved	N/A
1985	Highfield Commodities	Commodity broker/inv. mgt.	Wound up by DTI	3.12
1986	McDonald Wheeler	Investment management	Misuse of client funds	4.30
1986	New Hampshire Inv. Mgt.	Investment management	Wound up by DTI	0.16
1986	Global Guarantee Life	Investment management	Wound up by DTI	N/A
1986	London Investment Office	Container Leasing/inv. mgt.	Wound up by DTI	N/A
1987	Greenwood Inter'l Securities	Securities/inv. mgt.	Wound up by DTI	N/A

* N/A = not available.

SECTION 2   Fraud, Theft, and Irregular Dealings

2.1   The loss to investors from fraudulent activities depends on the type of fraud, on whether it is revealed, and on whether it leads to or is associated with insolvency of the management company. If the fraud is revealed and the company remains solvent, then the investor is likely to be fully compensated. In contrast, if the firm fails, client losses are dependent on how their funds were held within the company and, in particular, upon whether the funds were held in the company account, in an associated nominee company account, or with a third-party custodian.

2.2   The simplest division of fraud is between (a) employee fraud against the company, and (b) employee or company fraud against clients. A distinguishing feature is that, in the absence of financial failure, the first category imposes losses on the firm but does not necessarily affect the funds of investment clients.

Part A   Employee Fraud Against the Company

2.3   Employee fraud against a company can take several forms:

- stealing of company funds by employees;
- stealing of securities registered under the name of the company;
- stealing of other assets of the company;
- falsifying statements relating to, for example, expense accounts and purchases of equipment.

2.4   Little information is available on employee fraud, as most cases are resolved internally and receive little publicity. Significantly, from an investor's perspective, there have been no cases of fraud of this nature leading to financial distress and the ultimate collapse of an IM firm. More recently, however, several cases have come to light where the size of the fraud has involved many millions of pounds.

Part B   Theft or Misuse of Client Funds

2.5 This category of loss is of more direct concern to investors than employee fraud against the company, which must be addressed through internal controls and audit procedures by companies themselves. This second category of fraud exposes investors to direct potential losses. There are several groups of individuals in the firm who are in a position to commit theft against clients' funds: (a) salesmen, (b) employees who handle client accounts and assets, and (c) senior personnel or directors who can redirect client investments to own-accounts and accounts in other companies.

2.6 A common source of loss to investors has been the misuse of client funds by individual directors or senior personnel of IM firms. Two cases, McDonald Wheeler and Norton Warburg (covered in detail in the Appendix), are particularly insightful.

2.7 McDonald Wheeler was an investment management and financial advisory company that operated nine in-house investment funds worth £8.9 million, as well as managing individual clients' funds. The company was closed in July 1986 after a random supervisory visit by FIMBRA found a number of irregularities and deficiencies in the company's accounts. One activity that came to light was the investment of client funds in unsecured loans to private companies owned by or associated with the directors. This misuse of client funds was the basis for a writ served on the directors by the Receiver in the High Court. Separate company and client bank accounts had not been maintained, resulting in an estimated £5 million loss of client funds invested in the in-house portfolios. The in-house funds were operated like unit trusts, but the funds were held in the company account and thus did not enjoy the same degree of protection as separately held unit trust funds.

2.8 The collapse of the IM firm Norton Warburg in February 1981 was attributed to poor own-account investments by the company. In an effort to maintain solvency, approximately £4.7 million of client funds were diverted to associate companies in which Norton Warburg had a direct interest. A principal member of the company was gaoled for three years in 1987 on charges of fraudulent trading and false accounting relating to the transfer of clients' funds into the general Norton Warburg account. Significantly, investor funds were held in a nominee company within the group.

2.9 The failure of the nominee arrangement to prevent the transfer of funds in this instance suggests that strict separation with a third-party custodian controlling client bank accounts may be desirable. In the face of financial difficulties, the line between client and company funds is easily blurred, and the prospect of company failure provides an incentive to use accessible client funds to support the company's operation.

Part C Irregular Dealing Leading to Client Losses

2.10 Action may be taken that falls short of the theft of clients' funds but has the effect of benefiting investment management firms at the expense of their clients. A number of these activities would violate 'best-practice' guidelines, to the extent that they involve the investment manager transacting on behalf of the client, but not acting in the client's best interest. Instead, the agent may act in such a way as to extract a profit margin from the transaction at the expense of the client. Some of these activities represent ethical rather than legal violations of the investment manager's responsibility to pursue best practices, for example to obtain best prices, maintain the 'best' portfolio, and act in the clients' interests. Irregular dealing represents a non-contractual transfer of wealth to agents from investors. The following irregular or unethical dealing practices are discussed below: open account trading, 'soft dollars' or commission creaming, excessive trading or 'churning', backpricing of units, and portfolio manipulation.

Open account trading

2.11 Open account trading involves determining which of either the agent or the client will benefit from the transaction after the profit or loss associated with the transaction is known. Typical open account operations involve a fund manager giving instructions to a broker to purchase stock without specifying the end holder of the stock. The stock is booked to a suspense (or 'open') account of the broker's and is held there for a few days, pending subsequent price movements. If the price rises, the stock is then put through from the open account to the client's account at the new (higher) price. The profit is then transferred to another account by manufacturing bargains at the price at which the stock was traded through the open account. In this manner, profits can be transferred to beneficiaries of the agent at the expense of the client. If the subsequent price movement does not suit, i.e. if the price of the security falls, then the bargain is booked directly to the client concerned. The holding of purchased stock in a suspense account before 'booking' allows the agent to undertake later riskless trades on the basis of subsequent price information, and to extract profits that should rightfully accrue to the client.

2.12 A Stock Exchange investigation into the conduct of stock-brokers Halliday Simpson concluded that the firm had been operating an open account over a three-year period between 1978 and 1981 for the benefit of certain clients (see Appendix, case study III). The investigation concluded that Halliday Simpson had used its dealing suspense account as an 'open' account for the fund managers of some institutional clients. In particular, one of the users of the facility was Sir Trevor Dawson of the investment company, Arbuthnot Securities, who used the arrangement to benefit six beneficiary accounts. The parent company, Arbuthnot Latham, made a £340,000 compensation payment to the unit trusts managed by Arbuthnot Securities, and an undisclosed payment to other individual clients with funds under management. Such open account trading is extremely difficult to detect, and its operation by Halliday Simpson was uncovered only during investigations into an unrelated matter.

Commission creaming and 'soft dollar' arrangements

2.13 Commission creaming, or 'soft dollar', arrangements involve the investment manager charging higher commission charges than those charged to the firm by the broker. The difference may or may not be used to transfer wealth from clients to the investment management firm. In general, the incentive for commission creaming involving loss exists where the client pays broking charges separately from the investment management fee, rather than paying one fixed, all-inclusive management fee to the firm. In the former case, a loss may occur if a higher brokerage fee is charged to the client than that paid by the IM firm. In the latter case, the investment manager has an incentive to minimize all operating expenses, including brokerage charges.

2.14   The size of the IM firm may allow it to negotiate a discount with its broker, or the firm may be able to gain a lower rate through economies of scale achieved by grouping small orders into block trades before dealing. A distinction might be drawn between the firm obtaining (and not passing on to the client) a discount that could be obtained by any other firm acting for this client and one that relates to this one firm's superior efficiency.

2.15   Individuals too may benefit from 'commission creaming'. For example, fund managers may be offered incentives and rebates to place orders through particular broking operations. These rebates may be paid in kind rather than in cash. Other 'soft dollar' arrangements may involve the provision of computing facilities, research, etc., to the IM firm by a broker in exchange for business. While some of these arrangements are straightforward overhead reallocations, others may involve genuine benefits to the IM operation. Whatever the case, such arrangements may tend to commit the investment manager to deal through a particular broker and thereby diminish the energy with which he seeks the best prices for clients. These arrangements may involve breach of 'best execution' requirements.

Churning

2.16   'Churning' is the term used to describe heavy trading of portfolios to generate excessive management fees. Losses to clients arise not only from the increased management fees payable, but also through the less efficient management of clients' portfolios. Like many other forms of non-contractual wealth transfer, excessive trading is difficult to detect and prove.

Backpricing

2.17 A number of investment managers interviewed claimed that it was not unknown for unit trust managers to request trustees to create units at prices that prevailed at dates preceding their creation. This 'backpricing' may be carried out to take advantage of recent price movements. Unit trust managers cited postal or administrative delays as reasons for the backdating. However, it was argued by some that trustees were too willing to accept these types of explanations. Trustees, on the other hand, denied that this was happening or that it was widespread.

Portfolio manipulation

2.18 Investment managers may manipulate portfolios to present a more successful picture of a particular fund's performance. For example, unwanted stock may be sold to clients, and securities may be transferred between funds to achieve a more attractive position for portfolios that a firm wishes to promote. Interviews suggested that when a firm sponsored a new unit trust, securities may be shifted between trusts to the detriment of older established trusts. McDonald Wheeler, for example, was reputedly involved in trading investments internally between its different in-house portfolios that enhanced profit performance.

Part D: Established with the Intention of Earning High Returns

2.19 A number of companies have been set up with the express intention of earning large profits from speculative investment activities.

2.20 Miller Carnegie Securities was a London-based commodity options trader registered in the Bahamas. The firm employed about 20 personnel engaged in telephone sales of international commodity market investments. Miller Carnegie was closed down by a court order in July 1981. Clients had invested an estimated £750,000 with the group, of which less than a third was reported to have found its way into commodity contracts. In June 1981 the *Sunday Times* revealed that Michael Hart and Joe Tritt, both of whom were involved in the running of the company, had previous criminal records for fraud. At the 1983 trial of five men connected with the company on charges of conspiracy to defraud, the trial judge directed the jury to acquit for lack of a well-defined legal requirement that investors be accurately advised of the market prices concerned.

2.21 Greenwood International Securities Ltd were licensed dealers which were compulsorily wound-up by the High Court in June 1987. The company, a member of FIMBRA, had been operating for one year and had approximately 2,000 clients. Greenwood had strongly advised clients to invest in two private Canadian companies, Multi Choice Communications and Campbell Boys Industries. The winding-up petition presented by the Department of Trade and Industry stated that Greenwood's advice to clients had not been impartial as it had bought the shares for its own account. The DTI alleged that Greenwood had therefore acted in breach of its fiduciary duty to its clients.

2.22 Examination of the cases listed in Table 4.3 suggests that operations of this type usually display one or more of the following characteristics:

- short periods of operation;
- low levels of initial capital;
- the sale of complex or specialized investment products;
- 'hard sell' marketing techniques;
- overseas-based operations;
- the involvement of individuals lacking strong reputations.

Short period of operation

2.23 A large number of companies survive for only a short period of time, as they either leave the industry or are compulsorily wound-up by the authorities. For example, McDonald Wheeler traded for four years before a random supervisory visit by a FIMBRA inspector led to its closure. Imperial Commodities and Cornhill Securities each lasted less than two years, and others were operational for only a year or less. Most of the companies in Table 4.3 were wound-up on petition to the courts by the Department of Trade and Industry. In the case of Cornhill Securities, a commodity dealer, the company disappeared in 1984 after a series of changes of address. Clients had apparently handed over cash in exchange for contract notes purporting to show purchases of silver and other commodities by Cornhill on the New York Stock Exchange.

2.24 The brief period of operation of a number of these companies has important implications for monitoring and for the most appropriate regulatory response by the authorities to such operations. In particular, it suggests that new firms with no established reputation may require closer monitoring during their initial period of operation.

Complex or specialized investment products

2.25 Some companies in this category appear to specialize in technically complex or highly specialized products. Such products tend to have the characteristic that subsequent performance is difficult to establish. Speculative investment in more complex commodities, for example, appears relatively common in this category. (Miller Carnegie, Imperial Commodities, Cornhill Securities, and Highfield Commodities were all cases of firms involved in commodity broking.) It was noted in the Gower Report that 50 commodity trading groups had been under police investigation in late 1983. It is likely that products on which information is less readily accessible, or which are less readily understood or interpreted by the 'average' investor, may provide greater opportunities for companies aiming to maximize company or individual returns at the expense of the client.

'Hard-sell' marketing techniques

2.26 'Hard-sell' marketing techniques typically fall into two types of activity: one involves extensive use of glossy brochures and other advertising material aimed at promoting the 'professional standing' or 'reputation' of the company; the other uses high-pressure sales techniques such as unsolicited (or 'cold') home and telephone calling. In the first example, the company's credibility and respectability is often underlined with the prominent use of industry memberships, such as NASDIM or FIMBRA. McDonald Wheeler, for example, used such acronyms extensively in all its advertising and had inserted 'NASDIM' in the company's name. During the winding-up of McDonald Wheeler, it became apparent that advertising had the desired effect, with many clients believing that membership implied credibility and a guarantee of security. The responsibility of FIMBRA, and the absence of a compensation or insurance fund, came under close public scrutiny in the wake of McDonald Wheeler's failure.

2.27 'Cold' calling and repeat telephone calling have also been commonly used techniques in these operations. Miller Carnegie and Greenwood International Securities each employed about 20 telephone salesmen.

Overseas-based operations

2.28 A number of speculative IM firms that have operated in the UK in the past have been registered overseas. For example, New Hampshire Investment Management Ltd was registered in Cyprus, Miller Carnegie in the Bahamas, and Global Life in Panama. Highfield Commodities was registered in the USA and run by Americans, but operated out of the UK.

Prior personal records of IM managers

2.29 A number of individuals involved with the companies listed in Table 4.3 had previously been associated with failed companies. For example, John Wheeler of McDonald Wheeler had been declared bankrupt in Scotland. He had also been a director of two companies which had been placed in liquidation on grounds of insolvency. The frequency of such cases underlines the importance of applying 'fit and proper' tests.

Part E   Prosecutions for Fraud

2.30   One potentially serious concern is that fraud may possibly be encouraged by low rates of prosecution. According to the Roskill Report, of 247 inquiries conducted by the DTI under Section 447 of the Prevention of Fraud Act (1984), the following actions were taken:

- 73 were passed to other agencies for consideration;
- 59 were cleared on the grounds of insufficient evidence;
- 98 were found to contain evidence of misconduct, but no further action was taken;
- 9 prosecutions were undertaken, of which 7 cases resulted in convictions.

While not all of these case related specifically to investment fraud, the figures suggest that the overall rate of prosecution is low.

2.31   Fraud Squad figures support this picture, showing a low ratio of convictions to arrests. There are a number of reasons for the low conviction rate. One of the most basic is the extreme complexity of many cases, and the consequent difficulties faced by the prosecution in presenting evidence in a form that is comprehensible to a lay jury. This was a concern of Professor Gower, who advocated the introduction of a form of judiciary panel comprising both legal and (lay) financial experts. The resource costs involved in pursuing cases are high, and, while the Fraud Squad in general aims to have cases completed in 12 months, resource constraints have in the past delayed prosecutions for periods of up to 18 months after the initial investigatory work has been performed.

2.32   The constraints on enforcement and low probability of conviction reduce the disincentives to fraud. Furthermore, a number of the activities described in this section which enable the non-contractual transfer of wealth to investment managers are not illegal in terms of existing law. A fine line exists between illegal and unethical practices, and this has not been assisted by the lack of a well-defined legal system. Some of these ambiguities have been resolved by implementation of the Financial Services Act, for example the separation of clients' funds.

SECTION 3   Established Companies and Groups that Experienced Financial Distress

3.1   Investors may be exposed to losses in the absence of fraud if the IM firm, or the wider group of which it is part, experiences financial difficulties that lead to insolvency.

3.2   This section considers examples of financial distress, in which client funds have been placed at risk owing to the failure of the agent. Part A considers instances in which IM firms experienced difficulties as a consequence of being parts of larger groups, and Part B covers cases where IM firms themselves were in trouble.

Part A   Financial Distress in Groups Controlling IM Firms

3.3   A large proportion of client funds at risk during the secondary banking crisis (Table 4.2) were exposed to financial difficulties elsewhere in the group. Two prominent cases during that period were those of Jessel Securities and Slater Walker Securities, described in Appendix case studies V and VI, respectively.

3.4   Jessel Securities was a public listed investment company with diversified interests in fund management, property, and insurance and with a large industrial shareholding base. The group's difficulties stemmed from its insurance subsidiary, London Indemnity and General. The insurance company suffered a large outflow of funds from its guaranteed income bonds in 1973 caused by high interest rates and unusually favourable redemption terms. The parent company found itself fiancially constrained after asset prices collapsed and it was unable to meet a £6 million capital call from London Indemnity in late 1974. Increased capital was required to meet any further potential outflow of funds and to meet stricter Department of Trade and Industry capital requirements. The group set about a programme of asset disposals which included the sale of its unit trust business, Jessel Britannia, to Slater Walker in November 1974. Clients in the 16 Jessel trusts, which had a collective worth of £42 million, experienced very low disruption costs, and no funds were lost as a result of the difficulties stemming from the insurance subsidiary.

3.5   Slater Walker Securities experienced similar difficulties to Jessel's during the period 1975–7. Slater Walker's investment business was heavily involved in banking, insurance, property, and investment management, with approximately £300 million of funds. Under the chairmanship of Jim Slater, the group had been involved in a number of complex dealing arrangements which, coupled with some non-performing investments, led to financial difficulties. Falling prices during the secondary banking crisis led to losses in the group's property company, requiring heavy provisions in the banking operation which had been run as an 'in-house' bank. The Bank of England provided a standby credit facility to support the banking operation, and the group embarked upon a programme of asset and property disposals. The investment management part of the banking company remained profitable. In August 1977, the banking arm was sold to the Bank of England in a reconstruction plan and three loan stocks were redeemed, releasing the group from financial liabilities which were constraining its ability to borrow. The investment management group was renamed Britannia Financial Services and the insurance subsidiary Arrow Life. Both were regrouped under a renamed holding company, Britannia Arrow Holdings. Despite the financial difficulties, no client funds were lost and investors experienced relatively few disruption costs.

3.6   The key point in both cases was that there were no investor losses, as the IM division was either easily sold or reorganized into a separate profitable entity. Some other groups experienced similar difficulties during the secondary banking crisis, and the result was either a transfer of ownership or a reorganization involving relatively low disruption costs to clients. Examples included the J. H. Vavasseur group, Triumph Investment Trust,

Dawnay Day Group, Keyser Ullman Holdings, Cedar Holdings, and First National Finance Corporation.

3.7 The J. H. Vavasseur group had interests in banking, insurance, and investment management. In 1973–4 it experienced a run on its insurance subsidiary at the same time as it had to make heavy banking provisions and writedowns in relation to property sector commitments. The group's investment management interests included Vavasseur Unit Management and First Investors. Both of these companies were profitable and were sold to Henderson Administration in late 1974.

3.8 Triumph Investment Trust had a controlling interest in the National Group of Unit Trusts, which managed ten trusts worth a total of £92 million in 1973. It also owned Oceanic Unit Trust Managers Limited, whose ten trusts managed assets of £13.2 million in 1973. Triumph Investment's pre-tax profit of £2.1 million in 1973 was transformed by the declining equity and property prices into a loss of £19.5 million in 1974 after provisions and writeoffs of £21 million. The company collapsed in November 1974, and the investment management interests were sold by the receiver in 1975. The National Group interests were purchased by Slater Walker and the Oceanic Trusts were acquired by Lamont Holdings.

3.9 Dawnay Day Group acquired control of the Target Group in 1972, which included Target Trust Managers Limited and their Scottish subsidiary. In 1974 the group managed £47.5 million in 13 different funds. The banking subsidiary of the group was affected by the secondary banking crisis and survived only with the assistance of the Prudential Assurance. The banking activities were reduced, and in 1980 Dawnay Day was taken over by a subsidiary of Rothschild Investment Trust.

3.10 Keyser Ullman Holdings owned Key Fund Managers, which had £1.8 million under management in four funds during 1974. The group also had property interests and a secondary bank, Keyser Ullman. In 1974 the group was forced to obtain support from the 'lifeboat committee' (the bank rescue committee set up by the Bank of England during the secondary banking crisis) and at one point had £65 million of support loans outstanding. By 1976 all the loans were repaid, and in 1980 the group was taken over by the Charterhouse Group.

3.11   Cedar Holdings owned Cedar Fund Managers Limited which managed three funds. The holding company's investments were affected by the secondary banking crisis, and in December 1973 it announced severe liquidity problems. Institutional share-holders injected new funds and the group's principal banker, Barclays, provided support loans of up to £72 million. These loans were repaid in the following few years, and in 1979 Cedar Holdings was taken over by Lloyds and Scottish. The IM operation, Cedar Fund Managers, had however been sold to Gartmore Fund Managers in 1975.

3.12   First National Equities Limited was a subsidiary of First National Finance Corporation and had £1 million worth of funds under management in 1974. The parent company was severely affected by the secondary banking crisis and received loans of £350 million from the 'lifeboat committee'. An extensive programme of asset realization was undertaken, and the unit trust management company was sold to Hambros in 1975 with no loss of client funds.

Part B   Investment Management Companies in Financial Distress

3.13   In this part, the financial difficulties involve the IM operation rather than other activities within the group. Both unit trust holders and clients with funds under management have been exposed to the risk of failure by IM firms. In the first instance, the position risk of a number of unit trust managers during the secondary banking crisis exacerbated the financial problems caused by declining unit trust incomes. In the second instance, own-positions of IM firms have led to the failure of the company and the loss of client funds.

3.14   Some of the most serious problems of the 1973–5 period affected unit trusts. The problems were two-fold. First, the value of the funds under management fell in line with stock market values, thereby reducing fee income; and second, sales of new units declined. The drop in sales was particularly serious for the smaller management companies. In August 1973 net sales of unit trusts amounted to £8.97 million, of which £6.95 million was accounted for by the six largest management groups. The remaining £2 million of sales were shared among the other 75 management companies in the industry. A number of small unit trusts therefore experienced difficulties during the period.

3.15 Portfolio Fund Managers, for example, experienced a sharp reduction in asset sales and management charges, from £2,838,796 in 1972 to £994,693 in 1973. Successive losses of £14,651 and £19,723 were then recorded, and in early 1975 the trusts managed by the company were transferred to Piccadilly Trust Managers. Portfolio Fund Managers commenced winding-up proceedings in April 1976. The London Wall Group of Unit Trust Managers, which managed four funds worth £9.3 million in 1974, also experienced financial difficulties and was acquired by the Tyndall Group in early 1975. Likewise, Surinvest Fund Managers Ltd, with £4.3 million under management in three funds, was acquired by Schlesinger Trust Managers in November 1973. The transfer of IM responsibility in each of these three cases was achieved at no cost to clients.

3.16 Client funds managed outside of unit trusts have also been exposed to own-position risks of the IM firm. In particular, investor losses have occurred where own-account trading losses and non-performing investments have led to failure. The failure of the commodity broker M. L. Doxford is a case in point.

3.17 Heavy trading on its own account eventually forced M. L. Doxford out of business in 1981 (see Appendix case study VII). The company had suffered most of the losses in 1978 through a subsidiary, M. L. Doxford (Bullion) Ltd, which specialized in trading precious metals. However, with the assistance of bank loan finance secured against property, the company was able to keep trading until 1981. Doxford had not maintained separate client accounts, so upon liquidation clients effectively became unsecured creditors. Consequently, clients lost £1.133 million as a direct result of Doxford's own account trading losses.

3.18 Similarly, as previously discussed, trading losses contributed to Farrington Stead's build-up of debt to its broker, Hedderwick's, and led to the IM firm's default, while poor investment in financially dependent companies by Norton Warburg led to the misappropriation of client funds and the failure of the company.

3.19 A striking observation is that investors who had invested funds through separate autonomous investment management arms of larger groups, or unit trusts, have lost relatively little as a result of financial distress. This may be directly attributed to the separation of control of client accounts and securities from the IM firm to independent trustees.

SECTION 4   Lessons from the Past History of Investor Loss

4.1 This chapter has examined cases of financial distress in the investment management business that placed investors at risk of financial loss.

4.2 The amounts of money reported as lost by investors have been comparatively small, although the outcome of recent cases may affect this conclusion.

4.3 Most of those losses have occurred as a result of client funds being (a) stolen, (b) used to cover irregularities, (c) used to support losses on own-positions, or (d) required to meet operating losses. These losses to investors occurred primarily because the company had control over client funds even when those funds were formally separated from those of the company.

4.4 Such losses may have been avoided if third-party custodians had control over client accounts. It is striking that the theft of client funds has not occurred in unit trusts where custodian accounts have been used.

4.5 Reported losses of investors from fraud, theft, and irregular dealings may greatly understate actual losses incurred. Fraud is detected usually when the IM firm is in financial distress or is subject to investigation by a regulatory body. The latter may follow investor complaints or a random visit. Irregular dealings are much less easy to detect. For example, we found some concern about backpricing of units by unit trusts, but evidence was difficult to obtain.

4.6 Many of the failures occurred in companies that (a) operated for short periods, (b) had low levels of capital, (c) offered complex or specialized investment products, (d) operated from overseas, and (e) involved individuals lacking strong reputations. The attention of the regulators may usefully be concentrated on firms with these characteristics. ·

4.7 Some concern was expressed that the low level of prosecutions in the face of theft and irregularities may reflect a lack of definition of the law. Some of these practices, such as co-mingling client funds with company funds, have been clarified as a result of IMRO's rules.

4.8 Where financial failure was not accompanied by fraud, theft, or irregular dealings, investors suffered little loss of funds and disruption costs were low or negligible. In such cases the assets of the IM firms were quickly redeployed, and continuity of investment management services was maintained.

APPENDIX: CASE STUDIES

I McDonald Wheeler Fund Management Ltd

Summary

1 McDonald Wheeler Fund Management Ltd, a four-year-old investment management and financial advisory company, was compulsorily wound up in the High Court in 1986. The company was closed after a random supervisory visit by FIMBRA in July of that year had uncovered irregularities and deficiencies in the Canterbury-based company's accounts. In particular, separate bank accounts had not been kept for client and company funds, paper profits had been generated by internal transactions between funds, and client funds were invested in associated companies. Investors lost an estimated £5 million in the in-house portfolios operated by the company, and an initial writ claiming repayment of client funds was served on Mr and Mrs Wheeler. The writ asserted a breach of their fiduciary duty with respect to the transfer of client funds to associated companies. A warrant for the arrest of Mr John Wheeler on charges of fraud was issued. The prominent visual use of McDonald Wheeler's NASDIM and, later, FIMBRA memberships in promotion of the company, in addition to the principal's past record of invovement with insolvent firms and failings, focused attention on the entry requirements of the industry.

Company Profile

2 McDonald Wheeler Fund Management Ltd was formed in March 1983 as a private limited company with a paid-up capital of 100 £1 shares. John Wheeler with 51 shares and John Wilson with 49 were the two original shareholders and directors of the company. The company commenced trading on 1 January 1984, when it acquired the assets and liabilities of McDonald Wheeler Ltd. That company had been formed in June 1982 to acquire the partnership business of McDonald Wheeler Associates involved in

insurance broking, investment management, and financial advisory services. Of McDonald Wheeler Ltd's £20,000 authorized share capital, the £100 paid up was divided between Wheeler (49), Wilson (34), and Joan Hall (John Wheeler's wife) (17). In the first six months of operation to end December 1982, McDonald Wheeler Ltd made an after-tax profit of £222 on a turnover of £38,567. This was followed by a loss of £879 in the year to end December 1983, despite turnover being up to £121,424. After its acquisition, the company became a nominee company holding shares and other securities for clients of McDonald Wheeler Fund Management Ltd. Its name was accordingly changed to McDonald Wheeler (Nominees) Ltd in June 1984.

3 McDonald Wheeler Fund Management Ltd's authorized share capital was increased by 19,900 shares in November 1984, and 10,400 were issued for cash to Wheeler, Wilson, and Hall. Authorized capital was further increased to £200,000 in December of the same year, and another 94,500 shares were allocated for cash between the three directors. In the year to end December 1984, the company, now trading under the name of McDonald Wheeler Fund Management, made an after-tax profit of £14,942. Turnover, representing income generated via commissions and management fees, totalled £350,844, while expenses amounted to £308,603, including expenditure of £71,000 on advertising. At that stage the company had four wholly owned subsidiaries, each with a paid up capital of £100. These were System Hex Ltd, McDonald Wheeler Unit Trust Management Ltd, McDonald Wheeler (Nominees) Ltd, and The Investment Centre (Canterbury) Ltd, the latter acting as the retail outlet for the group.

4 The two principal directors, Wheeler and Hall, jointly owned two-thirds of the £150,000 paid-up capital at the date of the company's last annual return in September 1985. In contrast, John Wilson's shareholding had remained low, at 5,000 shares. At the time of winding-up in August 1986, the company had expanded to include ten associate companies. Mr Wilson had retired from McDonald Wheeler in 1985 owing to ill health.

5   The principal activity of the company was the management of nine in-house investment funds. Clients were attracted to these funds through a variety of advertisements and brochures. Accounts for the year ended December 1985 reputedly put funds under management at £25 million, of which £13 million had been invested in nine in-house funds by approximately 1,500 clients. Between 1,100 and 1,200 clients were still with the company when the receiver was called in, investing £8.9 million in the 'in-house' funds. Other business conducted by the firm included selling life insurance, pension plans, dealing in securities for individual clients, and providing venture capital.

Cause of the Difficulties

6   The problems of McDonald Wheeler were exposed after a random supervisory visit by a FIMBRA inspector in July 1986 discovered irregularities in the company's accounts. Dealing was suspended, and the company ceased to accept funds on 28 July. FIMBRA, with the agreement of the company, brought in an independent firm of accountants, and their report was later referred to the Department of Trade and Industry. The High Court was then petitioned by the DTI for the winding up of McDonald Wheeler, 'in the public interest', under Section 440 of the Companies Act (1985). An official receiver was appointed on 7 August 1986, and a Mareva injunction was granted to the receiver enabling him to freeze and seize assets without the defendants being informed. The compulsory winding-up order was granted in the High Court on 28 October 1986, at which point the receiver told the court that he regarded the company's affairs as a major failure and that nearly £5 million of investors' money had been lost.

7   In the Official Receiver's letter to clients of 20 September 1986, the extent of the company's activities were outlined. The company had failed to keep separate bank accounts for each of the nine managed funds and for individual investment clients. The accounting records that had been kept were totally inadequate, and it was difficult to ascertain precisely what assets had been acquired for which fund or individual investor. The only accounting records prior to October 1984 discovered by the 'special manager' were those contained in a cash book. These, however, did not analyse receipts and payments between each of the managed funds and, reportedly, only reproduced information in the company's bank statements. A computerized accounting system had been installed by McDonald Wheeler in October 1984 in an effort to maintain fund and client records. However, the receiver's investigations suggested that not all the entries that passed through the bank account were put on to the system. Moreover, certain entries processed on the computer records did not pass through the bank account and, according to the receiver, did not appear to be substantiated by external documentary evidence. It appeared that no reconciliation between the computerized records and the bank balance had ever been undertaken. There was also evidence of investments being traded between funds to generate internal profits.

8   Instead of investing the majority of funds in publicly quoted securities as advertised, only £1.8 million of the £8.9 million invested in the in-house portfolios had been invested in quoted securities and externally managed funds. A significant amount (£4.2 million) had instead been invested by way of share capital or unsecured loans in private companies. A number of these companies were owned or associated with McDonald Wheeler and controlled by John Wheeler and Joan Hall. These companies included: VIP Air Ltd, a private airline which never flew; Parkhill Engineering, which purchased a yacht for chartering valued at £150,000–£200,000, which was never chartered; and Ballachulish Enterprises, owners of a Scottish hotel. Other ventures included a Brighton boat showroom, a Marylebone property development, and companies owning property in Spain and Ireland.

9   At the winding-up hearing in the High Court, counsel for the DTI said that the in-house funds were effectively unit trusts, but the investors had not been told how their money was being invested. The funds were of a 'speculative nature' and did not enjoy the safeguards given to investors in authorized unit trusts.

Outcome of the Failure

10 Only an estimated £4 million of funds was recoverable from the in-house funds. Investors were expected to receive substantially less than 47 pence in the pound, which was to be distributed on a 'common pot' basis. All investors were to receive the same proportionate refund irrespective of which of the nine funds their money had been invested in, as the absence of adequate records precluded an exact identification of individual investments. The extent of losses on the individual client funds under management that were not invested in the in-house portfolios is unclear. McDonald Wheeler's professional indemnity insurance provided no protection against criminal default by John Wheeler.

11 The legal side of the case remains unresolved, not least because Wheeler and Hall are in the Republic of Ireland. A writ was issued by the Receiver against these two for the repayment of McDonald Wheeler's client funds. The writ sought a declaration that the Wheeler's transfer of money and assets from McDonald Wheeler Fund Management Ltd to ten associated companies was a breach of their fiduciary duty. The associate companies were quickly placed into receivership, and Ballachulish Enterprises was served with a writ seeking £100,000 repayment of salaries and loan capital.

12 The Receiver was also concerned with Canterbury-based Excess Insurance, which was unwilling to pay out on a professional indemnity cover of £1 million of McDonald Wheeler. Excess Insurance successfully claimed that the policy was void against criminal default by John Wheeler as he had failed to disclose 'material facts' about his business history. It appears Wheeler had previously been bankrupt in Scotland and had paid only a small proportion of his debts. He had also been a director of two companies that had been placed in liquidation on grounds of insolvency.

13 At the time of the creation of self-regulatory bodies under the Financial Services Act, the closure of McDonald Wheeler brought the performance of FIMBRA under close scrutiny. While the auditing process of FIMBRA had resulted in the closure of an 'unfit and improper' operator, the body was subjected to some criticism for granting McDonald Wheeler membership in the first place, in the light of John Wheeler's previous business history. It appears that a large number of investors believed that membership of associations like FIMBRA implied credibility and a stamp of approval. McDonald Wheeler, as with others, was quick to exploit this perception and used the acronyms prominently in advertising its investment management services. Indeed, the company went as far as to insert NASDIM in its logo, and stated prominently on the first page of its 1984 Annual Report that: 'McDonald Wheeler Fund Management Ltd is a member of NASDIM The National Association of Security Dealers and Investment Managers—and as such is approved by the Department of Trade and Industry to deal in securities.' The marketing of the company's image in this manner had the desired effect, with many clients believing that FIMBRA operated an insurance fund or was liable for compensation claims. Legal action against FIMBRA was considered, but not pursued, by a client committee of investors.

14 In summary, the case of McDonald Wheeler demonstrates the advantages of requiring a third-party custodian to handle clients' money, and the dangers of less formal arrangements which give the appearance rather than the reality of separation. In this case, clients' funds were managed like unit trusts, but were not protected by any of the safeguards, such as independent trustees, that are enjoyed by unit trust holders. The existence of such safeguards reduces the opportunities for manipulation and mis-appropriation of clients' funds by the IM firm. Professional indemnity insurance provided no protection against criminal default by the owner of the business. Furthermore, the previous business record of the principal, John Wheeler, underlines the importance of 'fit and proper' tests designed to identify potentially inappropriate operators prior to entry. The effectiveness of surprise inspections by regulators is also highlighted by this case.

II   Norton Warburg Group Ltd

Summary

1   The announcement in February 1981 of the voluntary liquidation of the Norton Warburg Group (NWG), a 'mainstream' and respected investment management firm, sent shockwaves through the City establishment and heightened calls for a review of investor protection.[1] Losses of clients' funds amounted to £4.5 million, and Andrew Warburg, the principal of the company, was gaoled for three years in 1987 on charges of fraudulent trading and false accounting between October 1978 and March 1981. The charges related to the transfer of clients' funds into the general NWG bank account. These funds had been misappropriated in order to maintain the solvency of the company after the withdrawal of funds by a major client in September 1978, and to support ill-fated investments in associated companies.

Company Profile

2   Andrew Warburg, a chartered accountant, left an insurance broking firm in February 1973 to set up Norton Warburg Ltd as a financial services company. He was accompanied by Melvin Perera and six other former employees of Scott Warburg and Partners. Peter Howland joined the newly formed company two months later and these three, along with Richard Stanes (who joined the board in 1975), were the key shareholders and directors throughout the period of operation of Norton Warburg.

3   Norton Warburg Ltd's share capital was stabilized at £15,000 in June 1974. Reserves were later capitalized in September 1977 (17 for 3 bonus) and September 1978 (1 for 1 bonus); and, together with a cash subscription in June 1978 and small share issues in 1979 to acquire two financial companies, issued capital rose to £262,000 at the time of the last company accounts to June 1979. Significantly, of this amount, only £24,400 had been issued for cash, while £237,600 had been capitalized from reserves. At that balance date

---

[1] The company has no connection with City merchant bank S. G. Warburg.

Andrew Warburg held 34.5 per cent of the issued capital, Perera 18.7 per cent, Howland 16.5 per cent, and Stanes 16.3 per cent.

4 Authorized capital was increased to £2.5 million in January 1980, and a further £27,600 capitalization of reserves (1 for 13.49 bonus issue) occurred in May 1980, along with a £110,400 cash subscription at £1.25 per share. More shares were issued in exchange for the whole issued capital of Norton Warburg Guernsey Ltd (£11,500) in early June 1980, and this was followed by a private cash placement of £1.28 million of shares in a new holding company, Norton Warburg Group, in July 1980.

5 NWG was involved in unsuccessful merger talks with several companies in early 1980. In particular, Mr Michael Ashcroft, chairman of Hawley Leisure and Provincial, and Mr Ronald Shuck, a Birmingham businessman and chairman of the London and Liverpool Trust, both considered involvement with the company. A firm of chartered accountants had investigated Norton Warburg on behalf of one party, and Mr Shuck, commenting on meetings between himself and the company, was reported as saying that he had received unsatisfactory answers from Norton Warburg. The failure of these talks led to the private placement of 1.28 million £1 shares in the Norton Warburg Group in July 1980. While the company had hoped to raise £1.75 million, the majority of shares had been placed with leading financial institutions, including Save and Prosper Group (400,000), Scottish Amicable Life Assurance (150,000), Scottish Amicable Pension Investments (50,000), and Tyndall Unit Trust (50,000).

6 Before the formation of the Norton Warburg Group, Norton Warburg Ltd, which was renamed Norton Warburg Holdings in 1979, had remained the parent company of the group since its incorporation. Norton Warburg Ltd offered financial counselling services geared to high income earners, insurance, and pension advice. Initially, investment management played a relatively small part in the company's operations, and it was not until the company became a licensed securities dealer in 1975 that formal management agreements were signed with clients.

7 During 1976–7 funds under management grew rapidly, and the balance of the company shifted in favour of investment management. By the end of 1977 the company had £8 million under management, and nearly £1.2 million of cash was being held for individual clients, none of whom, it was reported, had formal agreements for their deposits. Interest was credited to investment clients at clearing bank seven-day deposit rates on the amount stated as 'cash on deposit'.

8 As an emerging company, its 1977 Annual Report stated that its principle activities were:

(a) investment consultants, advisors, and managers;
(b) leasing of plant, machinery, equipment, and motor vehicles;
(c) insurance broking;
(d) provision of financial services.

At that time, Norton Warburg had 11 subsidiaries in which it held majority or 100 per cent share ownership, along with two unconsolidated subsidiaries, TFA Electrosound Ltd and Hornmark Ltd.

9 By 1979, Norton Warburg Investment Management had taken over the IM responsibilities from Norton Warburg Ltd and begun issuing investment management agreements with clients. The intended separation of client funds from company monies was explicit in the wording used in the agreements. In particular,

all cash and other assets will be registered in the name of Lloyds Bank City Office Nominees Ltd or such other nominees of similar standing as may in the absolute discretion of the managers be deemed to be necessary or convenient in an account designated Norton Warburg Investment Management Ltd Client Account.

10 The company suffered a setback in September 1978 when Pink Floyd, a successful music group, withdrew its management agreement worth £860,000 from the company. The group had been Norton Warburg's largest client throughout the first five years of operation and was also involved in a number of Norton Warburg offshoots, such as the former venture capital arm, Norton

Warburg Investments Ltd. (Pink Floyd indirectly held approximately 20 per cent.) Despite the loss of its largest client, funds under management continued to grow, and by the end of 1979 these totalled £11 million. Of this amount, £2.9 million was stated as 'cash on deposit'. At the time of the company's collapse in 1981, it was managing £12 million for approximately 370 clients.

11 Among the many subsidiaries of Norton Warburg Holdings, the three main companies were Norton Warburg Investment Management, Norton Warburg Ltd, and Norton Warburg (Nominees) Ltd, which was the vehicle for the majority shareholding in the unconsolidated subsidiary TFA Electrosound. Norton Warburg Investment Management had offices in California, London, and Guernsey. The group made an after-tax loss of £10,852 in its first 16½ months of operation to end June 1974. This was followed by a further £727 loss in the 18 months to end December 1975. Thereafter, the group experienced three successive periods of profit: £62,370 in the 18 months to end June 1977, £190,170 in the 12 months to end June 1978, and £171,023 in the year to end June 1979. The group bankers were Lloyds, while the auditors were Turquand, Barton Mayhew and Company (later merged into Ernst and Whinney) and Midgeley and Company.

Cause of the Difficulties

12 By the end of the 1970s, Norton Warburg was firmly established in the city and was well regarded as a firm of investment managers. Among institutions allowing Norton Warburg to advise their pensioners and employees were the Bank of England, the BBC, Unilever, and British Airways. Against such a background of respectability, and in the light of the 1980 share issue to leading institutions, moves to place the group into voluntary liquidation in February 1981 were greeted with surprise in the City.

13 As the company's affairs were unravelled, it became apparent that non-performing investments in subsidiaries, in particular in TFA Electrosound, placed the company in financial difficulties which were accentuated by the loss of its largest client in 1978.

Indeed, Andrew Warburg was reported in the press as attributing the company's collapse to the £2-million-plus investment in the Electrosound business. Similarly, Mr Vivian Robinson, QC, defending Warburg in court, maintained that the company had been honestly and properly operated until October 1978, at which point, it was claimed, it was insolvent. Insolvency may have also been influenced by Pink Floyd's withdrawal of their contract worth £860,000, placing the company, according to Robinson, in a 'very difficult position'.

14 Norton Warburg acquired a 73.5 per cent interest in TFA Electrosound Ltd in April 1976 for £19,083. Electrosound UK, as the company was known, was based in the UK and specialized in supplying sound equipment to pop music groups. Known formerly as Electrosound Productions Ltd, other shareholders of Electrosound included Mr Rikki Farr, and the company operated a wholly owned subsidiary, ESP Lighting. The audited accounts of Electrosound for the 18 months to end June 1977 showed a profit of £5,651. However, these were qualified by the auditors with respect to the amount of fixed assets in the balance sheet. Norton Warburg initially viewed its involvement with Electrosound as transitory, stating in the 1977 accounts that control of the company was intended to be temporary, and for that reason Electrosound's accounts had not been consolidated. Two other associated companies, Hornmark Ltd and Mrs Howie Ltd, were treated in the same manner in the accounts. The group's shareholding in Electrosound, however, was increased to 82 per cent in 1978 when Norton Warburg Nominees Ltd subscribed to 12,933 £1 shares issued by Electrosound.

15 Norton Warburg's involvement deepened via the establishment of TFA Electrosound Hollywood Incorporated in 1977, registered in the USA. An offshoot of Electrosound UK, 'Hollywood' was set up by Rikki Farr to supply sound and lighting equipment to musical groups in the USA. A new company, Sparmanor Ltd, registered in the UK and holding 49.5 per cent of the issued capital of Hollywood, was set up in November 1977 with Warburg, Perera, and Howland among its directors.

16 It appears that Norton Warburg's involvement with the music industry was financed with the use of client funds. The first of several transfers of funds from client accounts held at Lloyds Bank City branch to Norton Warburg's own company accounts at Lloyds Bank, Threadneedle Street branch, occurred in July 1977. Between July and October 1977, £550,000 was withdrawn from client accounts and deposited in the company's own account. A financial appraisal undertaken by Robson Rhodes after liquidation showed that approximately £4.7 million of clients' funds had found its way into the company account between July 1977 and 1981.

17 The movement of funds within the group and heavy funding of subsidiary operations by the parent are reflected in the company accounts. At the date of the last balance sheet, June 1979, Norton Warburg Holdings owed its subsidiaries, mainly Norton Warburg Investment Management (the arm managing client portfolios), £2.175 million. This figure was substantially larger than the amount owed to subsidiaries at each of the four previous balance dates (effectively zero). The use of these funds is reflected in the other side of the accounts, where the amount owed to Norton Warburg Holdings by Electrosound UK had steadily increased from £460,576 in 1977 to £826,876 in 1979. The amount due from consolidated subsidiaries also rose, from £10,093 in December 1975 to £653,607 in 1977 and doubled to £1,281,029 in 1979. Sundry debtors of Norton Warburg Holdings also increased sharply between 1978 and 1979, from £376,045 to £1,066,840.

18 Throughout the period, Norton Warburg provided various credit guarantees for Electrosound UK, which in turn was affording Electrosound Hollywood credit facilities at commercial rates of interest. By January 1978 it was estimated that Norton Warburg had lent Electrosound UK and Hollywood about £1 million through various sources, despite poor performarnce by Electrosound UK and no positive returns by Hollywood. In March 1978, Sparmanor Ltd issue £900,000 of unsecured loan stock at £95 per £100 stock. Of this, Norton Warburg Holdings subscribed to £167,000, and 120 clients of Norton Warburg Investment Management took £611,800 or two-thirds of the stock. Clients' funds were also invested in companies connected with Norton Warburg such as Landcrest, dealing in property, and Norton Warburg Investments (later renamed Waterbrook), a venture capital offshoot. (The latter investment vehicle, under Norton Warburg management, proved to be unsuccessful, with only one out of ten investments being profitable.) Shareholders, who had originally paid a premium for their equity, were expected to receive between 8p and 40p in the pound upon winding-up.

Outcome of the Failure

19 The history of NWG provides an example of where own-investment positions by the IM firm performed badly and caused failure, and client funds, which were supposed to be protected by being separated from those of the company, were then misappropriated to support the business operations.

20 The exposed financial commitments of the group were first highlighted by auditors Turquand, Barton Mayhew & Co. when they qualified the June 1977 accounts. In particular, they expressed reservations about the recoverability of advances to consolidated subsidiaries and of the amount due from clients. Turquand, Barton Mayhew & Co. were replaced in 1978 by Midgeley & Co.

21 In December 1979, seven directors resigned, led by Richard Stanes. Their action was prompted by a realization of the grave liquidity problems of the company. The failure of the company to attract a merger partner in early 1980, particularly after investigation by accountants, may be identified as another warning signal. Around the time of the placing of shares, £400,000 was paid to Norton Warburg Investment Management client account and £90,000 was paid back to depositors of Norton Warburg Ltd. Other money was passed to Electrosound Hollywood and a £157,000 interest-free loan was made to Mrs Warburg. While these payments reduced the money owed to clients of Norton Warburg Investment Management to £1.8 million, the directors of that company expressed concern about ability to repay the amount owed to clients 'in a reasonable period'.

22 At the time of liquidation, Norton Warburg Holdings owed £4.7 million to unsecured creditors. This was partly made up of the unsecured creditors of Norton Warburg Ltd and Norton Warburg Investment Management, who, reportedly, were owed £1.203 million and £2.73 million, respectively. Liquidators estimated a £4.6 million shortfall on client accounts at that time. The approximate statement of affairs indicated that, of a book value of £5.1 million, only £827,000, or one-sixth, was expected to be realizable. This was later revised downwards to £560,000. Electrosound UK was placed in receivership and its assets realized only £200,000, while Electrosound Hollywood proved to be worthless.

23 Clients of Norton Warburg can be divided into three major categories:

(a) those who had deposited money with Norton Warburg Ltd;
(b) those who were able to identify their portfolios with Norton Warburg Investment Management through statements of account;
(c) those who had portfolios with Norton Warburg Investment Management but were unable to identify them.

The 181 investors in the second category were paid in full, while investors in the third category received between 55p and 60p in the pound. Clients who invested through Norton Warburg Ltd received nothing. The total loss was in the region of £4.5 million, while further client losses were sustained on involvement with Sparmanor Ltd, Waterbrook, and Landcrest. The loan stock of Sparmanor, for example, purchased for £95 dropped to £15, representing a further loss to clients of £515,000.

24 During the creation of the new parent company in July 1980, a debenture was issued by Norton Warburg Holdings to Norton Warburg Group covering all finance passing from the Group to Holdings secured against a charge on all the assets of Norton Warburg Holdings and its subsidiaries. This had the effect of passing the £1.28 million raised in the private placement of shares in the Group down through the rest of the organization in exchange for paper. The validity of the debenture was contested by the Group and Holdings liquidators. James Clement, senior partner of Robson Rhodes and joint liquidator of Holdings, refused to recognize the validity of the debenture. He claimed that part of the money purported to be secured by the debenture was advanced before the debenture was issued, at a time when the directors of both companies knew that Norton Warburg was insolvent. Furthermore,

It was part of an unlawful plan made at the time of insolvency which, contrary to the whole basis of company law and equity, could result in the shareholders, including the directors who were responsible for the plan, being preferred to the creditors, the great majority of whom were investment clients and a large part of whose funds the directors themselves had improperly used.

The liquidators of Norton Warburg Group conceded that the debenture was not valid, and thus relinquished the Group's shareholders' potential prior claim to Norton Warburg Holdings' funds over the unsecured creditors.

25 Andrew Warburg admitted fraudulent trading and false accounting between October 1978 and March 1981 and was gaoled for three years in June 1987. Mrs Barbara Mills QC for the prosecution said investors received quarterly accounts to show that their funds were intact, 'although the cash element of their portfolio had mainly been spent on keeping the company afloat'. An investigation by Robson Rhodes revealed that around £4.7 million belonging to clients of Norton Warburg had found its way into the Norton Warburg general bank account. It was felt by many in the City at the time that such withdrawals in round sums should not have gone unremarked upon by the banks. Accordingly, the liquidators of both Norton Warburg Holdings and Norton Warburg Investment Management decided to sue Lloyds Bank for breach of contract or negligence in transferring investors' money from the client account to the company account over the three-year period.

26 Further legal action was taken by the liquidators against the auditors Midgeley & Co. in September 1985. The auditors were being sued for alleged negligence over their failure to qualify the accounts in 1978 and 1979 after earlier auditors, Turquand, Barton Mayhew & Co., had qualified the accounts in 1977. Successful legal action was also taken by the liquidators against Melvin Perera, Roger Lynch, and John Tickett, claiming £400,000 for outstanding partnership fees, expenses, etc., for operating an accountancy partnership through the medium of the company. The judge ruled that a bogus partnership had been set up and ordered outstanding partnership fees to be paid into court pending the determination of the liquidators' claim. Pink Floyd also issued a £1 million writ against the companies and directors in the Norton Warburg group, alleging a loss topping £2.5 million and claiming negligence and fraud.

27 In summary, despite the stated intention of keeping client and company funds separate, the financial pressure of unsuccessful own-investments resulted in Norton Warburg using client funds to finance its own operations. Solvency appears to have been maintained after October 1978 only through false accounting, misreporting of client portfolios, and the misappropriation of client funds.

III Halliday Simpson—Arbuthnot Latham

Summary

1 In July 1981 Halliday Simpson, a Manchester stockbroking firm, was suspended from trading by the Stock Exchange Council, pending the outcome of an investigation into the firm's dealing style. The Exchange concluded that the firm had operated an 'open account' to the benefit of certain clients over a three-year period between March 1978 and March 1981. Four partners and two associate members were expelled from membership of the Stock Exchange for gross misconduct, and three other partners and one associate member were suspended or censured by the Exchange. Halliday Simpson had used its dealing suspense account as an 'open account' for some fund managers of institutional clients, holding orders in the account until subsequent price movements determined the end beneficiary of any profits or losses. One user of the facility was Sir Trevor Dawson, the chairman of Arbuthnot Securities, the investment arm of the merchant bank Arbuthnot Latham. The unusual aspect of this example of malpractice is that open account trading, like commission fraud, is extremely difficult to detect, and in this instance was only uncovered during investigations into an unrelated matter.

Background

2 The Stock Exchange investigation into Halliday Simpson's conduct of business began in March 1981, when the Chieftain Unit Trust group asked the council to examine certain share dealings that had been carried out within the group. This followed an internal inquiry by Chieftain into an unrelated matter and the dismissal of Mr Ian Hazeel, an investment manager, in September 1980 for alleged breaches of the Chieftain trust deeds. Details of Hazeel's personal dealings were handed over to the Stock Exchange, and that information sparked the wider investigation into Halliday Simpson. The senior partner at Halliday Simpson was Mr David Garner, and the stockbroking firm of seven partners was financially sound.

3 Sir Trevor Dawson, chairman of Arbuthnot Securities, the investment arm of Arbuthnot Latham, along with Michael Barrett, the managing director, held many directorships within the Arbuthnot group. Unit trust and investment management were important components of Arbuthnot's business, and in the 1980 report the non-banking business (which also included commodity dealing and insurance broking) contributed £1.12 million to the group's trading profit of £1.9 million. In 1981, Arbuthnot Securities had £140 million of funds under management, of which £51.7 million was in unit trusts and another £90 million was under management for private clients.

The Stock Exchange Investigation

4 The findings of the Stock Exchange investigation were posted in late July 1982. The report concluded that Halliday Simpson had been using its dealing suspense account as an 'open account', allowing some fund managers to book transactions to the account before specifying the end holder of the stock. Typical operation of the account involved a fund manager giving instructions to Halliday Simpson to purchase stock and book it to the open account. If the price rose, the stock would be put through from the open account to the fund manager's institution at the new (higher) price. Entries were then created in the books of Halliday Simpson purporting to represent bargains for a private client account of the fund manager (or a relation, or an associate) at the prices at which the stock had been traded through the open account. In this manner, profits were transferred out of the open account to beneficiaries of the agents involved in the transaction at the expense of the principal, or clients. If the price did not suit, i.e. if the price of the securities fell, the bargains would be booked directly to the client. The exchange noted that it was not unusual for profit payments on the transactions to be made in cash.

5   The investigation found several thousand entries in the 'open account', clearly indicating that it was being used as more than just a temporary booking for bargains and medium for the correction of dealing errors. The 'open account' had operated for three years between March 1978 and March 1981 and had apparently also been used for some irregular deals involving small, local stocks which were not easily traded. In the notice to members of July 1982, the Stock Exchange stated that some records of the firm had been destroyed intentionally in early 1981 after a visit by a member of the City of London Police Fraud Squad on another matter. Furthermore, after the Stock Exchange committee of investigation was appointed, a large number of file copies of contract notes were mutilated by the removal of the section showing the party with whom the bargain had been undertaken.

6   A further report was completed by the Stock Exchange council, and a statement was issued in late October 1982 detailing the transactions and parties involved in the use of the account. A prominent case was that of Sir Trevor Dawson of Arbuthnot Securities. As a friend of the senior partner, David Garner, Dawson had placed substantial orders with the firm. It was

frequent practice for his orders to be placed in the 'open account' after execution in the market. Operation of the account as outlined above resulted in substantial surpluses when prices were favourable. These surpluses were then transferred to one of six client accounts by the manufacture of a pair of bargains, using the same security title and the same prices at which the 'open account' had purchased and sold the shares.

7   Both Dawson and Barrett, his deputy at Arbuthnot Securities, were suspended from executive duties in July and resigned in September 1981. Following an internal investigation into the personal dealings of Dawson and Barrett by auditors Peat Marwick Mitchell, it was announced in December 1981 that the unit holders in the trusts run by Arbuthnot Securities were to receive a special lump-sum payment of £340,000 from the company, made by means of a one-off addition to total funds. This amount was approved by the trustees, the Royal Bank of Scotland and Clydesdale Bank, as being more than sufficient to cover any losses. Undisclosed payments were also made to a small number of other investment clients for whom Arbuthnot managed funds.

8   The Stock Exchange investigation also concluded that four other clients had access to the open account facility operated by Halliday Simpson. These included Mr Ian Hazeel, who had been at the centre of the Chieftain investigations; Mr Bruce Dawson of Kuwait Investment Office; Mr Denis Little, an investment manager with Coutts & Co.; and an account operated in the name of Smith Forshaw & Harper.

9   The Halliday Simpson case is particularly interesting as it provides a rare insight into the operation of one of the least detectable forms of conduct that results in client losses. Operation of the 'open account' allowed those agents with access to it to 'cream' profits off the top of transactions without the principals (clients) being aware. Indeed, the uncertainties of the timing of orders, prevailing market prices, etc., would make it next to impossible for clients to detect such margin creaming on individual deals. The probability of detection by the client is clearly reduced

further in cases of unit trust or fund management. The fact that the 'open account' ran undetected for three years, and was exposed only in the process of unrelated investigations, bears testimony to the extreme difficulties involved in combating this type of conduct.

IV Farrington Stead–Hedderwick, Stirling, Grumbar and Company

Summary

1 On 10 April 1981, the stockbroking firm of Hedderwick, Stirling, Grumbar & Co., was 'hammered' after its bank, National Westminster, dishonoured cheques of the firm totalling £3 million. Hedderwick's failure resulted from counterparty exposure to Farrington Stead, an investment management group which owed £1.9 million to Hedderwick from unsettled gilt dealings. Farrington Stead's default on this outstanding debt appears to have resulted from a combination of trading losses and difficulties encountered in reconciling different creditors' conflicting claims on the firm. The subsequent untangling of both companies' affairs revealed excessive turnover of client funds by Farrington Stead, with the *Financial Times* estimating that the total commissions paid to Hedderwick implying an annual turnover in the order of £50 million on approximately £5 million of client funds. The clients of Farrington Stead recovered £1.15 million (92 per cent of funds under management in 1981); unquantifiable wealth losses resulted from the high commission costs associated with the firm's excessive trading levels. Although Hedderwick recovered little of the outstanding debt owed to it by Farrington Stead, the partners' assets covered all its outstanding liabilities.

Company Profile

2 Farrington Stead was a Manchester-based IM group which began operations in January 1979. It specialized in gilt trading and offered portfolio management services to clients. The group applied for a licence to deal in securities in January 1980 and had approximately 120 clients with £1.2 million under management at the time of its default to Hedderwick. The two principals in Farrington Stead were Geoffrey Farrington and Harry Stead.

Agnello de Souza was a registered shareholder between January 1979 and May 1980, and he provided a direct link to Hedderwick. De Souza had joined Hedderwick as part of a gilts team headed by Terence Webster in 1975 and, at the time of the default, was manager of Hedderwick's gilt-edged settlement office.

3   Hedderwick's had been experiencing difficulties and was in the process of concluding a rescue merger with the stockbroking firm of Quilter, Hilton, Goodison & Co. at the time of the collapse. Terence Webster, former partner and head of the Gilts Department, was expelled by the Stock Exchange in February 1980 after a 15-month Exchange investigation charged that he had

acted in a 'disgraceful manner' and 'contrary to the best interests of certain clients of the company in not obtaining the best possible market prices for clients' but instead acting to benefit certain discretionary accounts. He is also said to have concealed from Hedderwick that a certain discretionary account was being operated wholly or in part for his personal gain. (*The Times*, 7 February 1980)

Four other members of the firm were disciplined by the Exchange, and all reportedly resigned. Hedderwick was again under investigation in June 1980 for allegedly lending gilts to the jobber Wedd & Owen, which had gone into voluntary liquidation. Hedderwick was cleared of any misconduct in its dealings with Wedd & Owen in January 1981, and, against this background, it was announced in late February 1981 that it was to be absorbed by Quilter.

Cause of the Difficulties

4   Farrington Stead's £1.9 million outstanding debt to Hedderwick was uncovered by accountants Touche Ross, examining the stockbroker's books in advance of the proposed merger. This discovery about the brokers' underlying financial position led to their bankers, Natwest, declining to honour £3 million of Hedderwick's cheques and the 'hammering' of the firm on Friday 10 April 1981. The £1.9 million sum outstanding, representing a combination of commissions payable and trading losses, left Hedderwick with insufficient funds to meet its ordinary obligations. When settlement of the firm's remaining transactions was completed after the default, the excess of Hedderwick's liabilities over assets was reduced to around £1 million, most of which was owed to jobbing firms. These remaining creditors were covered by the 22 partners' estimated assets of £1.3 million.

5   A writ was issued by Hedderwick against Farrington Stead for the £1.9 million unpaid debt, and the assets of the firm were quickly frozen. A large proportion of this amount (£848,000) was paid by Hedderwick through its settlements office to Farrington Stead on 11 March 1981. Farrington Stead admitted its £1.9 million liability to Hedderwick but claimed that the slightly over £1 million worth of funds held by the firm belonged not to the firm but to its clients. Campion & Co., solicitors acting for Farrington Stead, claimed that beneficial ownership of the funds invested in the company always remained with the original investor, with Farrington Stead acting only as their nominee. The conflicting claims of the clients and Hedderwick's liquidator were finally settled, with the clients receiving £1.15 million or 92 per cent of their original funds, and Hedderwick reportedly receiving approximately £175,000 from Farrington Stead.

6   Hedderwick's liquidator issued a writ against de Souza in April 1981 for £1,934,412, claiming damages for breach of duty and trust and/or negligence as manager of Hedderwick's gilt-edged settlement office. Although Campion & Co. claimed that de Souza was at no time involved in the management of Farrington Stead, de Souza eventually agreed to pay Hedderwick approximately £400,000 in an out-of-court settlement. Hedderwick's liquidator also took legal action against Terence Webster, and this resulted in another out-of-court settlement of £100,000 being agreed in April 1982. Finally, negotiations were entered into with Quilter over Hedderwick's £350 million private client business, of which Quilter had picked up approximately 80 per cent. At the time Hedderwick was put into liquidation, the takeover by Quilter had been well advanced, but not complete. Letters had been sent to Hedderwick's 6,000 clients recommending that they transfer their business to Quilter, which was to have absorbed most of Hedderwick's staff. As it transpired, Quilter took on 30 of

Hedderwick's staff and six former partners. It is not clear whether any payment was made for the proportion of the client base that transferred to Quilter, even though the merger was abandoned.

7   Although it ceased operations in 1981, Farrington Stead was not wound-up in the High Court until October 1986 on petition of the Inland Revenue (seemingly the only creditor remaining at the time), which was owed £43,046. The nature of the original liquidity difficulties that led to the company's default to Hedderwick did not emerge in any detail, and throughout the winding-up proceedings no suggestion was made of any misappropriation of funds by the firm. It became clear, however, that during the firm's two years of operation it had paid Hedderwick about £300,000 in commissions and brokerage fees. The *Financial Times* (22 April 1981) estimated that this represented an annual turnover of over £50 million on approximately £5 million of client funds.

8   The Farrington Stead–Hedderwick case illustrates two key points. First, it highlights the counterparty risks associated with clients' unpaid transactions. Hedderwick collapsed after building up a large exposure to an investment management firm that was experiencing financial difficulties. In this case, the broker allowed a client to accumulate large outstanding trading debts, seemingly without retaining as security against debt either securities purchased or monies received (in respect of sold transactions) on behalf of the client. The eventual default of the client led to the collapse of the broking firm, which appeared to have insufficient working capital at its disposal. Second, only after the default of the IM firm led to Hedderwick's collapse was an inappropriate relationship exposed, viz. the connection between the manager of the firm's back office gilt settlement operation (de Souza) and the sizeable settlements debtor, Farrington Stead.

V   Jessel Securities

Summary

1   Jessel Securities, a publicly listed investment company with diversified interests in fund management, property, and insurance, and with a large industrial shareholding base, ran into financial difficulties in the early 1970s during the secondary banking crisis. The group's liquidity problems arose from difficulties experienced by an insurance subsidiary, London Indemnity and General Insurance. After a rapid expansion of its income bond business in 1972, the insurance arm suffered a large outflow of funds requiring a capital injection from the holding company which it was unable to meet. This precipitated a suspension of the parent company's shares in October 1974 and a subsequent programme of asset disposals. Both the group's unit trust business and assurance subsidiaries were sold and a consortium of insurance companies took control of the insurance operation. The holding company went into voluntary liquidation in December 1975. All secured creditors were repaid, while unsecured creditors received about 30p in the pound. Despite the financial difficulties of both the holding company and its insurance subsidiary, there were no losses to client funds held in other subsidiaries.

Company Profile

2 The parent company of the Jessel Group, Jessel Securities, was formed by Oliver Jessel in the late 1950s as a private investment company. Jessel Securities came to the stock market in 1965 by way of an introduction, and although a private company, it already had about two hundred individual and institutional shareholders. The company quickly acquired four industrial concerns, and by 1970 it had begun a programme of company purchase and disposals, along the lines of Slater Walker.

3 By 1974 the group's interests ranged widely over both financial and industrial enterprises. Among its wholly owned subsidiaries were Jessel Britannia, the unit trust company, and two insurance arms, London Indemnity and General Insurance, and Life and Equity. The company had substantial mining and commodity interests, steel-making operations, and a 34 per cent holding in the engineering group, Johnson Firth Brown. Jessel had generally avoided banking and property, although it did hold 20 per cent of the banking concern, G. R. Dawes, and controlled a South African property and real estate company, Jessel Properties

(South Africa) Ltd. Investments in associate companies made a significant contribution to the profits of Jessel Securities, with 60 per cent of the £3.33 million profit in the six months to end December 1973 being derived from this source.

Cause of the Difficulties

4 Jessel's difficulties stemmed from its insurance subsidiary, London Indemnity and General Insurance, which had a life fund of around £85 million and 80,000 policy-holders. The insurance subsidiary had expanded rapidly in 1972, attracting £70 million worth of premium income into guaranteed income bonds. As interest rates rose in 1973, however, investors surrendered their policies in order to invest in higher-yielding bonds. Premium income plunged to £16 million, and withdrawals were believed to have reached £10 million a month at one point. By December 1973 the Department of Trade and Industry (DTI) and the Government Actuary's Department were concerned about the solvency of the company. Jessel Securities responded by increasing the share capital of the insurance subsidiary by £12 million, of which half, £6 million, was left as an uncalled liability on the parent company.

5 The strong outflow of funds continued until the Budget in March 1974 put an end to the tax advantages of guaranteed income bonds. Despite the stemming of the flow of redemptions after the Budget, the DTI, applying a stricter basis for asset valuations, was still concerned about the actuarial solvency of the company. It felt that the remaining guaranteed income bonds and other policies did not incorporate adequate penalties in the event of surrender. Jessel Securities, however, was experiencing financial difficulties of its own. The share market collapse had substantially reduced the value of its investments and equity base to the point where it was close to its borrowing limits, with the consequence that the company was unable to rely on its bankers for further borrowings. The difficulties were compounded by a £6.6 million loss in its South African property subsidiary in the 16 months to end June 1974. As Jessel Securities was unable to meet the £6 million capital call by its insurance subsidiary, London Indemnity was itself unable to sustain another potential run on its funds. The DTI therefore issued a statutory notice to the company that it was considering a ban on all new business, and a decision to stop writing business was taken by agreement. Jessel Securities' default on unpaid share capital call led to the company asking the Stock Exchange to suspend dealings in its shares on 15 October 1974.

Outcome of the Failure

6 Jessel embarked upon a programme of asset disposals under supervision of its financial advisors after consultation with its principal bankers, Barclays, Midland, and Hambros, and the trustees of a £10.1 million unsecured loan stock in the company's name. A rescue operation by a consortium of insurance companies led by Prudential Assurance took over the policies of London Indemnity. Attempts to save Jessel Securities, however, failed. The company announced in December 1975 that it was going into voluntary liquidation after a capital reconstruction scheme proposed by Hambros was rejected by the Receiver of London Indemnity, at that point the largest individual creditor with £6 million due in respect of the partly paid share capital. The asset disposals allowed repayment of nearly all the group's secured borrowings, but only approximately £8.3 million was available for an estimated £22.8 million of unsecured debt. Principal unsecured creditors were the holders of £10.1 million, 9¾ per cent, unsecured loan stock, London Indemnity (£6 million), and other subsidiary companies which were owed about £3.2 million. Jessel Securities had incurred capital and extraordinary losses of £40 million.

7 The difficulties within the group were confined to London Indemnity and the holding company; other subsidiaries and associates were not financially affected. Both the unit trust management group and the trustees of the funds, Midland Bank Trust Company, stressed that the unit trust subsidiary was unaffected by the difficulties. Jessel Britannia's 16 unit trusts had an estimated collective worth of £42 million in October 1974, and the amount invested in associated companies of the group was described as small in relation to the total funds under management. As part of the asset disposal programme, the unit trust arm was sold to Slater Walker for £1.58 million in November 1974.

Therefore no client funds under management were lost as a result of financial distress being experienced elsewhere in the group.

8 Similarly, Life and Equity, the other insurance subsidiary, was free from difficulties and was subsequently sold in the asset disposal programme. Significantly, the surrender values of Life and Equity's policies were linked to equity values and, unlike London Indemnity policies, carried no guaranteed component.

9 As with Slater Walker, the profitable and secure operations of the group were readily disposed of and clients' funds under management within the group were not at risk. In the absence of fraud or theft, the assets of the company were easily purchasable by another group. Investors experienced relatively low disruption costs as a result of the financial difficulties of the group.

VI   Slater Walker Securities Ltd

Summary

1 Slater Walker Securities Ltd experienced financial difficulties during the secondary banking crisis resulting in the disposal of its banking and property interests and rationalization of its investment management and insurance divisions between 1975 and 1977. The public company had emerged under the influence of its chairman, Jim Slater, in the late 1960s–early 1970s as a respectable investment banking and financial services group. The early years had seen the company involved in strategic position-taking in asset-rich companies and complex dealing arrangements within the group structure, with associates and third parties. The nature of such growth however placed Slater Walker in a vulnerable position in the early 1970s, and the secondary banking crisis exposed the company to financial difficulties. Heavy losses were experienced in the banking division, which had effectively functioned as an 'in-house' bank, while other losses were sustained on the group's property holdings. Jim Slater resigned in October 1975, and the Bank of England provided standby credit facilities to the banking division to back deposit withdrawals. Heavy bad debt provisions and increased capital requirements throughout the group, however, resulted in the eventual sale of the banking division to the Bank of England in August 1977. Despite significant withdrawals, the investment management and insurance arms of the group had remained profitable throughout. The sale of the banking division prevented the winding-up of the entire group and resulted in the loss of no client funds during the period.

Company Profile

2 Slater Walker Securities was formed in 1964 and in its early years specialized in buying industrial businesses with under-employed assets. Under the guidance of Jim Slater, one of the founders, the company quickly expanded to include a diverse range of industrial enterprises with wide international holdings in Europe, America, Australia, South Africa, and Asia. Jim Slater was credited in some quarters with contributing to a new and more positive approach among British managers to the efficient utilization of assets, while in others he was viewed as an 'asset-stripper'. Towards the end of the 1960s, Slater Walker's focus shifted to becoming an established investment banking operation with strong international links.

3 Slater Walker Securities was essentially divided into four operating divisions, comprising 'banking' (Slater Walker Limited), insurance (Slater Walker Insurance Company Limited), investment management (Slater Walker Investments Limited and Slater Walker Trust Management Limited), and property (Slater Walker Properties Limited). The holding company also held a range of equity stakes in other companies.

4 Just before experiencing financial difficulties, the group appeared to be performing well. The share price had peaked at 310p in 1972, and profits peaked in 1973 at £23.4 million with the impetus coming from the commercial banking operation. Earnings per share were 16.9p, the gross dividend 6.82p, and the group's equity was capitalized at £102 million by the market.

5 The turning point in Slater Walker's fortunes may be identified when a third attempt to merge the company into a substantial

'City' financial group failed in June 1973. Advanced plans to merge Slater Walker with Hill Samuel were aborted in the face of Hill Samuel executive opposition. Jim Slater responded by writing to shareholders stating that the board's objective was to become an international investment bank and that it intended to achieve that objective through internal growth. That set in train a policy of disposing of unsatisfactory foreign and domestic assets, and a shift into holding cash as 'the optimum investment'.

6   The retrenchment of Slater Walker showed up initially in the 1974 interim results. Creditors, deposits, and short-term loans were down from £303 million to £205 million as money market resources were steadily redeployed, and loans and advances fell as an effective freeze on new lending was implemented across the group. Net current assets were up from £39 million to £108 million, and unspecified realization losses were charged to reserves. Market equity capitalization had fallen to £70.5 million, although pre-tax profits had fallen only slightly to £10.1 million in the first six months compared with £11.9 million in the previous year.

7   The financial difficulties at Jessel Securities, which also operated a unit trust group and an insurance company, had an adverse effect on the share price of Slater Walker as public confidence weakened during the secondary banking crisis. In response, Slater Walker made a public statement in October 1974 detailing the liquidity position of the group's insurance and unit trust operations. In particular, Slater Walker noted that 37 per cent, or £21 million, of the insurance company's funds were being held in cash at the time, compared with a total surrender value of all income bonds of £27 million. (Redemptions of income bonds had created Jessel's problems.) Likewise, the group's unit trusts were 38 per cent liquid, with cash balances of £15 million being placed with leading banks outside the group by the trustees. With confidence in the group falling (reflected in a share price slide to 45p), Slater Walker injected £5 million of new capital into the insurance subsidiary, and the division's cash balances were then raised to £25 million.

8   By the end of 1974, Slater Walker had relinquished nearly all its overseas holdings and was continuing its policy of domestic asset disposals and balance sheet reduction. Profits slumped to £4.4 million in the second half of 1974, bringing the annual result to £14.5 million. A rigorous cutback in lending occurred in the second half of the year as the climate for banking/dealing operations turned progressively worse. Factors accounting for the profit decline were a £5 million decrease in associate company contributions (arising from disposals), mounting property losses, lower second-half dealing profits, and a flat year for corporate finance.

9   The extent of Slater Walker's financial difficulties emerged when the interim results for 1975 were declared in August 1975. Pre-tax profits for the six months fell to £2.2 million compared with £10.1 million in the previous year. Returns from investment dealing, traditionally the main source of income of the group, fell sharply from £6 million to £234,000. Commentators greeted this result with surprise, given Slater's past record and 'dealing touch', and at a time when the market reputedly had not been short of opportunities in the kind of dealing in which the company had previously excelled. Streamlining in the commercial banking activities resulted in a profit fall from £4.6 million to £2.5 million, while property losses rose sharply to £955,000 compared with those of £364,000 in the previous year. Investment management activities, on the other hand, returned profits of £700,000 compared with £825,000 for the whole of 1974. Market capitalization of the group continued to fall, down to £46.2 million; and, despite insufficient earnings to cover a recommended dividend of 4.15p per share (gross), the board committed itself to the maximum permissible dividend increase over the full year.

10   In October 1975, Jim Slater resigned as chairman of Slater Walker over allegations by the Singapore Stock Exchange regarding the operation of a controversial share incentive scheme in the Far East. The Exchange alleged that Spydar Securities, a company set up by six senior executives of Slater Walker Securities concerned with the Far East, made profits by buying shares at below market

prices in two Hong Kong companies, King Fung Development and
Kwan Loong (Hong Kong). The Exchange's investigation concluded
that contract notes purporting to show the purchase of the shares
contradicted the facts. Six executives had made personal profits on
the share deals of just over £1 million. However, as part of a settlement between Slater Walker Securities and Haw Par Brothers International in June 1976 over a disputed loan arrangement in which
Haw Par had purchased Kwan Loong, the six agreed to repay the
profits to Slater Walker Securities within five years.

11 In a move to protect his existing stake of approximately 8 per
cent in Slater Walker, James Goldsmith took over the role of
chairman after Jim Slater's resignation. This stake was later
increased to nearly 11 per cent with the acquisition of Slater's
personal holdings in early 1976. A new board was constructed in
October 1975 including representatives of the merchant banks,
N. M. Rothschild and Hambros. The new board cancelled the 1975
interim dividend declared in August and commissioned accountants
Pcat Marwick Mitchell & Price Waterhouse to undertake an
internal financial appraisal of the group.

12 That report, released to shareholders in September 1976,
highlighted the financial difficulties the company was facing. The
accountants were to a greater or lesser degree critical of the
management under Slater's chairmanship of every important
activity of the group. The exception was the investment management division, which appeared to be 'well run and managed in an
orthodox manner'. Of particular concern was the view that the
banking division was regarded as an 'in-house' bank, the use of
imprudent banking practices, the lack of provisions throughout the
group, and poor portfolio management in the insurance division.
The key characteristics of each division are discussed below.

13 *Banking Division* The 'in-house' nature of the banking
division resulted in £68 million out of total advances of £91 million
at the end of October 1975 being advanced to companies in which

Slater Walker had, or had previously had, an interest, or to individuals to finance shareholdings in such companies. The inherent weakness in the lending of the division was attributed to:

(a) a small number of very large loans whose size appeared out of proportion to the resources of Slater Walker Ltd: in particular, four loans accounted for 51 per cent of the portfolio, while 13 per cent of the 150 loans on the books accounted for 82 per cent of the portfolio;
(b) the fact that the terms of £36 million worth of loans included a provision for rolling forward interest;
(c) a mismatching of maturity dates of assets and liabilities.

Provisions of £29 million against the loan portfolio were required, and had it not been for Bank of England support arrangements, it appears that the banking division would have been insolvent. An initial Bank of England standby facility, secured in October 1975 to cover deposit withdrawals following Jim Slater's resignation, was extended in late November 1975 to £70 million, of which approximately £45 million was utilized.

14 *Property Division*   At end September 1975, the division comprised around 200 companies holding around the same number of properties. Despite the accountants' view that the property division's business had been conducted professionally, losses were being made and provision of some £14.8 million was recommended against the property portfolio. That portfolio had a book value of £75.3 million at the end of September 1975, of which 60 per cent was accounted for by ten properties. Most of the division's activities were funded by borrowings, amounting to £60.8 million. Of these borrowings, £47.8 million were in the form of intra-group indebtedness.

15 *Insurance Division*   Slater Walker Insurance Ltd was involved in both general and life insurance. General insurance had annual premiums of £12 million, while the life insurance side had £57 million in its long-term business fund with an annual premium income of £10 million. The main problems of the division identified by the investigating accountants were that the long-term

business fund's assets were not sufficiently well matched; that too
high a proportion of the investment portfolio was in the inflexible
low-yielding medium of property; and that there were too many
holdings of portfolio investments of questionable value. The
division was not contributing a dividend to the group as income
was being used to build up reserves to back increased redemptions.
The book value of Slater Walker Insurance was written down from
£11 million to £6 million.

16 *Investment Management Division*   This division drew together
a number of separate legal entities including Slater Walker
Investments Ltd and Slater Walker Trust Management Ltd. The
main activities comprised portfolio management for private clients
and certain group companies, UK unit trust management, and
offshore trust management. At the end of September 1975, the
division had just under £300 million of funds under management,
comprising:

● £40 million of private and institutional clients' money;
● £75 million of group funds;
● £170 million in UK unit trusts;
● £10 million in offshore trusts.

Significantly, only 2 per cent of funds were held in companies
connected with Slater Walker Securities, 1 per cent in clients of the
banking division, and 4 per cent in strategic holdings.

17   The unit trust group had expanded through acquisitions of
Jessel Britannia in November 1974 and the various funds of the
National Group of Unit Trusts in February 1975. Jessel Britannia,
acquired at a cost of £1.58 million, was one of the most profitable
subsidiaries of the troubled Jessel Securities Group and had 16
unit trusts under management. National Trust had around 20
trusts under management, and, together with the existing Slater
Walker trusts, the group managed 44 separate trusts. A rationalization plan, leaving nine trusts independent and combining the
remaining trusts specializing in similar investment fields, reduced
that number to just over 20 by the end of October 1976. The
estimated cost of streamlining the group was placed at £150,000.

18 In the opinion of the accountants, the investment management group was well run along prudent lines. The division's profit performance had reflected this, despite the unit trust business facing abnormally high levels of repurchases during the 'secondary banking crisis'. A detailed examination of the investment division by the merchant banks Rothschild and Hambros, completed in December 1975, also gave the division a clean bill of health.

Outcome of the Difficulties

19 In summary, the group was highly geared and in need of heavy provisions against a number of its activities. The total effect of all provisions was to reduce the net worth of the company from £80.9 million at end December 1975 to £40.7 million. The banking division was performing badly and was suffering under the company's previous dealing style. The property division continued to make losses, and the insurance division was not contributing to group profits. The disposal of property assets and general investments was stepped up, but the group's losses continued, with a £6.34 million pre-tax loss being recorded in the first six months of 1976.

20 The financial difficulties of the group were resolved in August 1977 when, faced with the redemption of three outstanding loan stocks, the banking division was sold to the Bank of England for £3.5 million. The terms of the loans, totalling £14.2 million, had placed a borrowing limit on the group which, if breached, would have led to the winding up of the whole group. The reconstruction plan also involved the purchase by the banking division of two of the most important property assets of the group, a $US convertible note issue and a £3 million tax loss payment to Slater Walker Securities.

21 The severing of the group's banking division and the disposal of its property and general investment interests left the group with its two strongest and most profitable divisions—investment management and insurance. These were renamed and grouped under a new holding company, Britannia Arrow Holdings (replacing Slater Walker Securities). The investment division was renamed Britannia Financial Services and the insurance division, Arrow Life. While emerging 'relatively' unscathed from the financial difficulties being experienced elsewhere in the group, there had been £18 million of repurchases by unit-holders, and the pension fund management activities had ceased to grow.

22   Client funds had been at risk to the complete failure of the group. However, in the absence of fraud, the disruption costs to investors were low in this instance. The separation of control of client funds to trustees and the autonomous operation of the investment division within the group provided investor safeguards against potential misuse of funds. The low investment of client funds in companies associated with the group highlights the benefits of strict separation in these cirumstances as Slater Walker had been involved in a number of complex dealing arrangements within the group and with its associates.

VII   M. L. Doxford & Co. Ltd

Summary

1   The commodity broker M. L. Doxford & Co. had been in operation for nearly eight years when it was announced in December 1981 that it was to go into voluntary liquidation. In the 18 months to October 1978, the company had sustained heavy losses trading on its own-account through M. L. Doxford (Bullion) Ltd. However, supported by bank finance secured against property, Doxford continued to operate for a further three years. Clients' funds had not been separated from company monies, resulting in a £1.133 million loss to clients upon liquidation. After extensive investigation by the Fraud Squad and the Department of Trade, no criminal charges were brought against Doxford & Co.

Company Profile

2   M. L. Doxford & Co. was launched in 1974 when Michael Doxford and four other employees of G. W. Joynson, a commodity broking group, set up on their own as agents for Bache, a leading US brokerage house. Describing itself in its annual report as a commodity broker and dealer, Doxford specialized in the management of portfolios and discretionary accounts for institutional and private investors. These activities were largely centred around the discretionary management of pooled commodity portfolios for syndicates comprising a minimum of five clients. The terms of the agreements entered into with clients gave Doxford full discretionary power to conduct 'the day to day business and management of the syndicate', and 'as managers of the syndicate shall in our name and ostensibly as principal, but in reality as agent for, and with the sanction of, the syndicate negotiate and enter into all contracts for the purchase of sale of commodities'. No management fees were charged, but syndicates paid commissions and brokerage fees on all transactions to the company. Clients were to receive a monthly statement and audited report of the syndicate's performance over a year. Agreements were to terminate if the number of syndicate members fell below five, the syndicate incurred a loss equal to or greater than 70 per cent of the initial capital of the syndicate, or on one month's notice.

3 On incorporation in January 1974, the company had a paid up capital of 1,000 £1 shares virtually all held by Michael Doxford (999). Issued capital increased to £6,000 in November 1974 when 5,000 shares were issued to M. Doxford (2,000), Jonathan Morley (1,500), and Nicholas Peto (1,500). Morley, who had worked in commodities for 14 years specializing in sugar and coffee, joined Doxford as managing director, while Peto joined as a director. Another 18,000 shares were issued to the three directors in June 1975, and this was followed in March 1976 by an issue of 76,000 shares at par for cash. In October of the same year, £900,000 was capitalized from the profit and loss account in the form of a 9 for 1 bonus. This increased the respective directors' shareholdings to 640,000 for Doxford, 150,000 for Morley, and 150,000 for Peto. Of the £1 million winding-up capital, £126,000 had been fully paid for in cash while £874,000 had been allocated through the capitalization of reserves.

4 During the first years of operation, Doxford was successful and clients made good profits. Although returns were highly variable, some syndicates were showing profits of 155 per cent by May 1976. The company's healthy returns were concurrent with a period of expansion: in the 18 months to September 1975, Doxford's net commissions receivable totalled £457,788; in the next seven months this figure increased to £506,005; and in the next 12 months to April 1977, to £1,990,690. Funds under management peaked at £8 million in 1977, and a new subsidiary, M. L. Doxford (Bullion) Ltd, was formed to trade in precious metals. By this time, M. L. Doxford Ltd's annual turnover had stabilized at around £2 million, but poor investment performance had already triggered a steady withdrawal of clients' funds. In the 18 months to October 1978, M. L. Doxford (Bullion) Ltd's turnover was £44,933,955, almost doubling to £83,831,000 in the following year.

5   By October 1979 the number of subsidiaries had grown to 13. While not all the companies traded, the group was involved in insurance broking, bullion dealing, property, and a variety of industrial businesses. It had representatives in the USA, the Far East, Bermuda, and Gibraltar, and regularly ran seminars for expatriates in the Gulf. The parent company was a member of the London Commodity Exchange and the International Commodities Clearing House. In 1979 Doxford sought legal advice on the implications for the company of the 1979 Banking Act. The directors accepted counsel's opinion that the prohibitions contained in the Act on accepting deposits did not apply to monies received by the company from clients in connection with the company's commodity investment services.

6   Despite the company's initial success in terms of client returns, its own-profit performance was less than impressive. After turning a trading loss of £25,477 in the first 18 months of the company's operation into a £4,314 profit in the next seven months, extraordinary expenses led to accumulated losses of £79,876 by April 1976. The positive returns on clients' portfolios and associated increase in turnover resulted in the company's only net profit (£34,494 in the year to operation). This was followed by dramatic losses of £1,965,729 in the year to October 1978 and a further loss of £191,000 the following year.

Cause of the Difficulties

7 The company's pre-tax losses of £2,010,722 in the 18 months to October 1978 coincided with the formation of M. L. Doxford (Bullion) Ltd. While the detailed nature of the losses did not emerge, Mr Peter Copp of accountants Stoy Hayward, commenting on the 'Statement of Affairs' presented to the creditors meeting in December 1981, was reported as saying that Doxford had made trading losses on its own-account of £1.5 million. It appears that the trading was carried out through M. L. Doxford (Bullion) Ltd, as the turnover of M. L. Doxford Ltd remained constant between 1977 and 1978 at around £2 million.

8 The trading losses put financial pressure on the firm and probably placed it in a position of technical insolvency. The company managed to finance the losses, however, through a loan facility of £1,750,000 obtained from Wilson, Smithett & Cope, a member of the Guinness Peat Group, secured by a charge over the company's leasehold property in St James Street, London. Doxford had purchased the property lease during the 1977 financial year for £849,717, and in July 1978 a new 99-year lease was negotiated at an additional cost of £437,899. After an independent valuation, the lease was revalued at £2 million, yielding a revaluation surplus of £1,153,635 in the 1977 accounts. Of the loan facility, £1,606,041 had been utilized at the end of October 1978 and the company's total interest bill had increased to £144,596, compared with £18,569 in the previous accounts. A second property valuation undertaken by consultant surveyors in August 1979 revalued the lease at £4 million, and the revaluation surplus was brought forward and included in the October 1978 accounts.

9 A period of worsening investment performance on clients' portfolios was associated with the company's losses in 1978 and 1979. After good results in early years, reported losses of some syndicates ranged from 8.55 to 68.92 per cent, and investment consultants with clients in Doxford began advising clients to reconsider their investments. As a consequence, Doxford experienced a net outflow of clients' funds, and by December 1981 funds under management had fallen to £1.133 million. The company's accumulated losses had risen to £2.13 million by the end of October 1979, and Wilson, Smithett & Cope had increased Doxford's loan facility to £2.5 million. The financiers continued to increase the loan over the following two years against the security of the lease, and were reported to have secured personal guarantees of up to £175,000 from Doxford's directors as late as October 1981. At the time of liquidation, Wilson, Smithett & Cope had a loan of £5,351 million outstanding to Doxford.

Outcome of the Failure

10 By the end of 1981, the financial pressures on the company could not be sustained; withdrawal of client funds was continuing and no extra loans could be raised. On 17 November, Doxford announced that it had ceased trading in commodities and hoped to sell the business and its headquarters. This statement was followed on 2 December by the announcement that the directors were placing Doxford into voluntary liquidation.

11 The estimated net liabilities of the company on liquidation stood at £2,857 million, which included a total of £1.133 million owed to 494 clients. Wilson, Smithett & Cope were owed £5.351 million secured against the leasehold property, while trade creditors were owed £234,960. Preferential creditors included the Inland Revenue, owed £105,000, the local authority, £36,000, and staff, who were due £11,000. Assets of the company were valued at £5.646 million in the liquidator's statement of affairs, including a £5 million valuation of the St James Street property. Of the respective creditors, Wilson, Smithett & Cope had recourse to the property (the realization value of which was uncertain), while preferential creditors (the Inland Revenue and secured debenture holders) were all paid in full. Unsecured creditors and clients, on the other hand, received no payment, despite initial suggestions at the December 1981 creditors' meeting that they were likely to receive 7 pence in the pound.

12 At that creditors' meeting, the press reported that the directors put forward five reasons for the company's failure:

(a) lack of computerization in the company's early years, which had led to inadequate monitoring of transactions when market conditions were hectic;

(b) poor trading in such market conditions, which had resulted in losses on both the company account and on its discretionary clients' accounts, some of the latter also being absorbed by the company as the losses exceeded the original funds subscribed by clients;

(c) sizeable bad debts;

(d) reduced turnover and high interest rates in later years;

(e) the company's inability to dispose of its property and other assets: this was seen as a solution to the company's liquidity problems and, according to Michael Doxford, it was the company's repeated failure to sell its West End offices (offered for sale at a price of £5.75 million) that led to the company's liquidation.

While the other factors may clearly have had some influence on the company's condition, the fundamental cause of the company's failure was the losses from trading on its own-account, mentioned under (b) above. Interestingly, the absorption of client losses suggested in (b) implies a breach of contract (see paragraph 2 above), as client syndicates were to be dissolved if losses exceeded 70 per cent of initial capital.

13 A question mark also exists in relation to the company's use of funds with respect to two subsidiaries, Limit Up Ltd and Doxford Freight Services Ltd. The former company owned a power boat raced by Mr Doxford at the company's expense, and the latter was formed as an import–export agency to transport the boat. Total sponsorship across the group as a whole amounted to £400,000. In addition, the group paid a total of £558,000 to directors in remuneration and spent a total of £155,000 on promotional expenses.

14 The size of the losses incurred by clients as a result of Doxford's failure strongly suggests that client funds were used to support and operate the company. As Doxford was not legally required to maintain separate client accounts, clients effectively became unsecured creditors upon the failure of the company, with the result that they had very little protection from company losses. The Doxford case further emphasizes the benefits of separating client funds from those of the company.

5 Different Motives for Regulation: A Survey of the Literature

SECTION 1   Introduction

1.1   There are three classes of literature that are relevant to a study of the regulation of investment managers. The first is corporate finance theory, which explains how a firm's capital structure is determined. The second is regulation of banks and in particular bank capital adequacy requirements. The third is the regulation of the professions. This chapter will discuss each in turn.

SECTION 2   Corporate Capital Structure

2.1   The design of a regulatory system that sets capital requirements has to take account of the capital structure that firms would choose in the absence of regulation. Regulatory systems that set requirements that are low in relation to a firm's chosen levels are ineffective. Regulatory systems that set high requirements can impose high costs on firms by forcing them to choose capital structures that are very different from preferred ones.

2.2   Risks associated with the running of a business will affect the costs of raising different forms of finance. For example, debt is priced at levels that reflect risks of encountering financial difficulties. Investors can earn safe returns by holding government securities and the debt of blue-chip companies. To induce them to hold more risky assets, higher interest rates will have to be charged as a compensation for risks of default on interest and principal obligations. If investors are indifferent to risk (if they are 'risk-neutral'), then the expected return from a high-risk investment will have to be equal to that on government securities or blue-chip firms. Interest rates offered will therefore be greater than those on government securities by just that amount that offsets expected costs of default. If investors are averse to risk, then interest rates on risky investments will have to include a further premium.

2.3 As a consequence, shareholders of risky firms are unlikely to earn greater 'risk-adjusted' returns than their riskless counterparts. The higher interest rates that shareholders have to pay when not in default offset the losses that they impose on creditors when they are in default. In that case capital structure is a matter of indifference. This is the basis for the well-known irrelevance of capital structure proposition that is associated with Modigliani and Miller (1958, 1963, 1969) and has been restated by Stiglitz (1969, 1974).

2.4 The important point to note from this description is that the mere existence of risk does not invalidate the irrelevance proposition. However, this sanguine view is undermined by one important characteristic of financial markets. The story that has been told so far assumes that, while different types of investors may differ in their perceptions about or attitudes towards risk, they are all equally aware of its existence. There are, in the parlance of the literature, no 'asymmetries in information' between different classes of investors; thus, all investors have exactly the same information. That assumption is unrealistic in many cases, and, as the next chapter describes, differences in information lie at the heart of many of the issues that concern regulators.

2.5 There are two classes of problems that asymmetries in information create. The first afflicts holders of corporate debt and the second, shareholders. Creditors receive fixed returns or, more precisely returns that are unrelated to the performance of the firm. Unlike shareholders, they do not benefit from high returns. But when performance is poor and there is a default on interest or principal repayments, they receive lower returns. Therefore, an increase in the riskiness of investments made by firms worsens the prospects of creditors even if the overall expected returns of firms are unchanged. In the face of such potential changes in risks, creditors are forced to monitor the behaviour of firms and impose restrictions on their activities. The greater the risk of this form of expropriation of returns from creditors and the higher the costs of 'bonding' firms to their creditors, the less willing creditors will be to lend and the lower will be the levels of gearing.

2.6 These incentive problems also afflict shareholders when they are not the managers of the firm. If equity is used to finance the operations of a firm, then the larger the outside shareholding of a firm, the lower the return to increased effort by the managers. As a result, managers will expend less effort than they would if they were shareholders.

2.7 A firm's capital structure therefore involves a trade-off between the bonding costs that are required to discourage firms from pursuing activities that are against the interest of their creditors and the 'moral hazard' problems that come from the use of equity finance (see Jensen and Meckling 1976). If there are penalties imposed on managers in the event of default, then debt can be used as a way of motivating managers and discouraging the slack that is associated with equity finance. High levels of debt act as a discipline on management by requiring strong profits performance to service payment of interest and principal (Grossman and Hart 1982).

2.8 A related set of theories regard capital struture as a method of communicating information to investors rather than as an incentive mechanism. If managers are better informed than investors about firms' prospects, then methods will be sought for communicating information to investors. Some have suggested that capital structure can perform just such a signalling function. For example, managers that are sanguine about prospects for their firms will be more willing to accept financial risks associated with high levels of debt than other managers. If managerial remuneration is related to investors' perceptions of the value of firms (through, for example, stock option schemes), then firms with buoyant prospects will wish to distinguish themselves from others.

Capital structure may be a means by which firms can do that. Optimistic managers will view the trade-off between the return to a bullish signal and the risks of higher gearing more favourably than more pessimistic managers. This is regarded as being particularly pertinent to the level of dividends paid by firms (see, for example, Bhattacharya 1979; Miller and Rock 1985; and John and Williams 1985; but see Edwards 1984 for a critique of this class of theories). In addition, it has been applied to the gearing behaviour of firms (see Ross 1977).

2.9 Asymmetries of information between investor and manager therefore affect firms' preferred financial structures for incentive and signalling reasons. The greater the moral hazard risks associated with equity, the more effective is debt in encouraging managers to conform to investors' goals. The more optimistic managers are about corporate performance, the greater is the information value of communicating buoyant prospects through high debt.

2.10 The important point to note is that, while asymmetries of information may influence firms' capital structure, none of the models referred to above suggests that governments can correct the distortions (moral hazard or bonding costs) associated with asymmetries of information. There is no case for government intervention.

2.11 The first suggestion that there may be public policy implications stemming from informational asymmetries came in a seminal paper by Stiglitz and Weiss (1981). This argues that the real problem that asymmetries create is that they undermine the operation of markets. It was noted above that, faced with a risk that firms may default, creditors will seek higher interest rates. If investors are uninformed about the quality of different types of firms, that is if asymmetries in information prevent them from discriminating between firms, they will attribute average quality to all firms. So high-risk firms that offer creditors poor prospects and low-risk firms that offer good prospects will all pay the same interest rate because investors are unable to distinguish between them. For the same reason that low-risk firms offer creditors good prospects, the owners of low-risk firms expect to earn less than the owners of high-risk firms. In fact, interest rates may be sufficiently high that it is not worth while for low-risk firms to stay in the market. In that case the market becomes populated by a large number of low-quality, high-risk firms; i.e., the bad drive out the good. Investors appreciate that the quality of the market is poor and demand still higher returns, which drives out even more high-quality firms. The market steadily declines as the quality of firms deteriorates.

2.12 This is an application to financial markets of a model of the used car market proposed by Akerlof (1970). In the secondhand car model, buyers are unable to establish the quality of cars. Given buyers' inability to determine quality, the average quality of cars on the market determines the price at which transactions take place. 'Lemons' reduce the average quality of cars sold and depress prices. Lower prices discourage owners of high-quality cars from putting their vehicles on the market, and average quality declines, leading to a further fall in prices. Information deficiencies in investment management and their implications for regulation of investment managers are pursued in Chapter 6.

2.13 Information may not be the only reason for the choice of particular financial structures. Recently increasing interest has been shown in the control aspects of finance (see for example Aghion and Bolton 1988, and Mayer 1989). These models place less emphasis on differences in risk between debt and equity and the incentives that they place on management, and more on the allocation of control between creditor and shareholder. Shareholders are not only the residual claimants on the firms' earnings (after other obligations have been met) but also the owners of the firms' assets. Therefore shareholders have the right to determine how a firm's assets are managed. Creditors do not have such a right, unless the firm is in default, in which case control may pass from shareholder to creditor. When should that occur? In terms of the deployment of the firm's assets, the appropriate point is when the shareholder has demonstrated that he is less competent than the creditor at running the firm. If the performance of the firm (reflected in its earnings) is informative about the ability of the shareholder (and his managers), then there will exist an optimal level of debt which determines a minimum performance of the firm, below which control is transferred from the shareholder to the creditor.

2.14 The value of the control models in this discussion is that they emphasize the important point that a preferred financial structure exists only where financial performance is related to the underlying quality of firms. If financial performance provided no information on the quality of management, then there would be no reason for using financial structure to effect changes in control. Other indicators—sales targets, productivity levels, qualifications of management, and quality of management systems—would be used instead. It is only where financial returns assist in distinguishing good from bad management that capital structure has a role to play. This will be a central consideration in establishing the appropriate form that regulation of investment managers should take.

SECTION 3   The Regulation of Banks

3.1 In contrast to non-bank financial services, there is an extensive literature on the theory and practice of bank regulation. Until recently, capital requirements on banks were considered in terms of the risks of bank insolvency. Optimal capital requirements were regarded as a trade-off between the distortions imposed on banks by requiring them to deviate from their preferred financial structure, and the risks of bank insolvency (see for example Santomero and Watson 1977). High capital requirements raise costs of capital for new and existing banks and thus discourage entry and competition between firms. Too low capital requirements impose excessively high risks of default on depositors. The more serious are the consequences of bank defaults, the greater will be the appropriate level of capital requirements.

3.2 Recently the financial failure to which banks are prone has been subject to more careful scrutiny. Diamond and Dybvig (1983) demonstrated that insolvency is not a necessary condition for bank runs. Perfectly sound banks can be subject to runs. The reason for this comes from the nature of bank assets and liabilities. Bank deposits are liquid and callable at notice. In contrast, bank assets are generally illiquid and are realizable only at substantial cost. Even if the value of bank assets is in excess of that of its liabilities, depositors may still choose to liquidate their deposits.

3.3 The incentive for liquidation comes from the procedures by which bank assets are distributed between depositors. Until insolvency is declared, a bank is required to meet withdrawals on demand. On insolvency, depositors join a pool of creditors whose claims are assessed by the courts. If a run occurs, only those who are at the head of the queue can expect to be paid in full. The mere risk that others will withdraw may therefore be enough to prompt a panic, irrespective of the underlying financial position of the bank.

3.4 Several solutions to the risks of runs have been suggested. Since the risk arises from the shortfall of the liquid value of bank assets below those of liabilities, runs can be avoided by requiring banks to hold assets whose net realizable value is in excess of that of liquid deposits. However, since the primary function of a bank is to transform short-term liabilities into long-term assets, the requirement that realizable value of the two be equal is very restrictive.   ·

3.5 Instead, deposit insurance has been proposed as a method of maintaining investors' confidence in banks, while allowing banks to continue to perform their transformation function. If full insurance is offered, then the incentives on investors to realize their deposits in advance of others will disappear. At most, depositors will suffer a temporary inconvenience of being unable to gain access to their funds straightaway. However, with anything less than 100 per cent insurance, incentives for premature withdrawal will still exist.

3.6　The problem that full insurance presents is that it creates inappropriate incentives on banks. If the government or a central bank provides insurance and the insurance is not properly priced, there is an incentive on banks to pursue unduly risky investments. If high-risk investments succeed, the banks' shareholders benefit. In the absence of insurance, if the investment fails, bank depositors suffer and they will require higher interest rates to compensate for this risk. But if the government offers full insurance, the costs of a bank failure are not borne by either the shareholder or the depositor: instead, the government pays the price of unduly risky investments.

3.7　There are two responses to this. The first is to monitor banks. Bank supervision is used as a method of evaluating the quality of bank portfolios and avoiding unduly risky positions. While monitoring can diminish incentives to defraud, it cannot eliminate them. The second is to price insurance. By relating the cost of insurance to the riskiness of bank assets, incentives to finance high-risk investments can be diminished. The problem is that insurance is difficult to price. Although regulators may be able to rank banks in terms of the riskiness of their portfolios, it will not be possible to determine the expected values of losses arising from default with any degree of precision. The pricing of insurance will inevitably appear arbitrary. Some have argued that this problem can be avoided by using private insurance markets instead of government insurance (see for example Kareken 1986). However, it is very doubtful that private insurance will be available to protect against systemic risks. Since 'runs' create risks of simultaneous bank failures, insurers could face devastating claims. As will be discussed in the next chapter, private insurance is more relevant to the idiosyncratic risks of investment managers than the systemic risks of banks.

3.8　In the light of the impracticality of most other alternatives, capital requirements are the form of protection that is most frequently proposed. The determination of capital requirements has for the most part been more a concern of practitioners and policy-makers than academics. However, the rules that policy-makers have chosen have been subject to extensive comment and criticism. The primary concern that has been voiced is that risk ratios which are commonly employed do not appear to bear a close relation to portfolio measures of risk (see for example Schaefer 1987). The ability to default is essentially a (put) option on the assets of the firm. Through limited liability, shareholders have the option of defaulting on their obligations to creditors. The value of these options increases with the risk of investments made by a bank and falls with the capital that the bank holds. To keep risks of default below certain levels, banks should be required to hold capital. But the amount of capital they are required to hold should be related to the overall riskiness of their assets in relation to their liabilities. If capital is to be required of institutions elsewhere in the financial sector, similar procedures should be used to determine the appropriate level of requirements.

3.9 In terms of the present discussion, the literature on capital adequacy for banks serves one useful purpose. It demonstrates that existing arguments for the regulation of banks relate to factors that are peculiar to banks. The structure of assets and liabilities of banks creates risks that may well not be present in other financial institutions and companies. In particular, the risk of runs arises from the specific function that banks perform of transforming liquid liabilities into long-term assets. That is why banks have been subject to special attention. No substantial case for the regulation of other financial institutions has been made to date. Furthermore, even if a substantial case does exist, the fact that banks face risks different from other companies suggests that appropriate solutions may also be different.

SECTION 4 Regulating the Professions

4.1 As subsequent chapters will describe, the third class of literature, which does not explicitly relate to financial institutions, is in many ways the most relevant to the regulation of investment management. Pursuing the market for 'lemons' theory that was discussed in Section 1, Leland (1979) argued that there may be a case for imposing regulatory requirements that set minimum standards. The argument is that the prices that suppliers receive for services they provide reflect the *average* level of quality provided, not the marginal level. Thus, so long as average quality exceeds marginal, there is an incentive for further entry to occur, thereby depressing the average level of quality supplied.

4.2   However, subsequent articles have emphasized the risks that regulation presents. Shaked and Sutton (1981) argue that self-regulating professions have an incentive to impose barriers to the entry of new members into a profession. Rents thereby accrue to existing members to the detriment of consumers, who are forced to pay prices that are in excess of those that would be charged by a more competitive industry.

4.3   In a similar vein, Shapiro (1986) demonstrates that, in professions that regulate entry, there will be a tendency towards overinvestment in training and the provision of high-quality goods. Where certification is used as a criterion for entry, potential entrants will be encouraged to undertake training to meet stipulated requirements. Those who require the provision of high-quality services may benefit from licensing and certification. But those who do not will lose out, because low-quality services will not be available at a low price.

4.4   This literature reminds us that, in seeking to correct distortions that may exist because of imperfections in the operation of markets, distortions of a different kind may be introduced. Regulation may cause supply to be unduly constrained. Certification and licensing overcome the quality problem that pervades certain types of markets only by curtailing the freedom of individuals to consume low-quality goods and services at low price. There is therefore too little choice and too much emphasis on quality. The solution that economists normally advocate is not restrictions on entry or regulation but improvements in the quality of information that is available to consumers. This idea will be pursued in the next chapter.

SECTION 5   Summary

5.1   Three classes of literature have been discussed: the capital structure of firms, the regulation of banks, and the regulation of the professions. These emphasize different issues that are relevant to the subsequent discussion.

5.2   First, the literature on capital structure suggests that risk *per se* does not present a problem. Returns will adjust to take account of the risks that are incurred by different classes of investors. Where problems do occur, they are frequently associated with differences in information available to different parties. However, while asymmetric information may give rise to particular types of financial structure, it does not of itself justify the intervention of a public agency. It is the effect of asymmetric information on the performance of a market that is of greater concern. The fact that high-quality firms may be driven out of the market may raise public policy questions.

5.3   However, the literature on self-regulating professions warns us of the dangers of regulating the quality of markets that are subject to asymmetric information problems. There is a tendency to over-regulation, and too much emphasis on the provision of high-quality services. Prices in general will be too high, and consumers will be unable to purchase low-quality services at low cost.

5.4   The literature on the regulation of banks reminds us that the issues that banks raise are quite different from those of most other parts of the financial sector. The problems of contagion and 'runs' that afflict banks are a reflection of the composition of their assets and liabilities. Insurance can be used to reduce the risk of runs, but problems of pricing can discourage its widespread application. Private insurance will not in general be available because of the systemic nature of the risks that can be encountered. Capital requirements are an important part of the regulation of banks because risks are largely financial. Control theories in corporate finance point to the direct relation between capital structure and the control of firms. Only where financial performance is related to the underlying quality of firms would we expect capital structure to be relevant.

5.5   These results will be applied to the regulation of investment management in subsequent chapters.

6 Market Failure and Investor Protection

SECTION 1 Introduction

1.1 The previous chapter described the rationale for the imposition of capital requirements on banks. This chapter examines whether similar considerations apply to investment managers.

1.2 The feature of banks that gives rise to a capital requirement is the holding of assets that are less liquid than liabilities. The potential shortfall in liquidation values of bank assets over liabilities creates risks of 'runs'. A 'run' develops when an insolvency of one bank precipitates withdrawals by depositors of solvent banks because they are unable to distinguish between solvent and insolvent firms. The run itself increases the number of insolvencies. Investment managers that hold client balances may be prone to similar disturbance. But if investment managers do not hold client balances, the bank model is not directly relevant. Notwithstanding, investment managers are subject to other risks that were described in Chapters 3 and 4. The questions they raised are, first, whether there are market failures associated with these risks and, second, whether capital adequacy requirements are the appropriate response.

1.3 The chapter is divided into eight sections. Section 2 lists the nature of the risks to investors arising from the IM process and the consequent costs that were described in Chapters 3 and 4. The costs to investors arising from these risks are (a) losses from theft and fraud; (b) disruption costs arising from default by the IM firm; (c) loss of client balances; and (d) uncompensated losses from the IM process.

1.4 In Section 3 the sources of market failure are explained. For example, in the case of fraud and theft, there is an incentive for investors to underinvest in monitoring the quality of IM firms. If the fraud does not coincide with default, the losses to investors may remain undetected and investors will remain uncompensated. If default occurs, investors will know *ex post* that a theft has taken place; however, this will not prevent losses. Since they will be unable to distinguish *ex ante* between the quality of IM firms, investors will require higher returns of IM firms in 'general, with the result that some honest IM firms will be driven out of the market and the IM process will be undermined.

1.5   Whereas Section 3 analyses market failures that are internal to the firm, Section 4 examines market failures arising from systemic risks.

1.6   In Section 5 alternative methods of correcting market failure are described. They include monitoring by private and public agencies, compulsory insurance (private or mutual), separation of clients' balances (with custodian accounts) and own-positions, and capital requirements.

1.7   Section 6 discusses the merits and deficiencies of these alternatives. This lays the foundation for relating the market failures of Sections 3 and 4 to different forms of investor protection in Section 7.

1.8   Section 8 summarizes the chapter's recommendations.

SECTION 2   The Nature of the Risks in the IM Business and the Costs to Investors

2.1   Chapters 3 and 4 described three classes of risk associated with the investment management business. These are summarized in parts A to C of Table 6.1.

Part A   Fraud and Theft and Non-Contractual Wealth Transfers

2.2   A distinction was drawn in Chapter 4 between firms that were driven into insolvency as a consequence of fraudulent activities and those that were not. In the absence of default, the investor is at risk if the fraud is not detected. In that event, losses may be imposed on investors which should really be borne by firms.

2.3 Irregular dealings include churning and the backpricing of unit trust units. They may also include non-contractual wealth transfers arising from a failure of firms to compensate investors for losses sustained by execution errors and settlement delays where those losses should be borne by the firm. These activities may be viewed as a form of theft on the grounds that their revelation would have encouraged clients to have shifted their custom elsewhere or changed the terms on which they were transacting.

2.4 Where default occurs, detection is not at issue. Instead, the risk to the investor is that, as a consequence of a financial deficiency, full compensation for fraud and theft cannot be paid. Even if compensation is paid in full, there may be disruption costs associated with an interruption to business. Cessation of business may temporarily deprive the investor of proper portfolio management.

2.5 Levels of fraud recorded in Chapter 4 were, for the most part, small. However, these figures do not include losses that occur in the absence of default. Furthermore, it is quite conceivable that future losses from fraud, theft, and irregular dealings will be larger than those in the past. Recent deregulation of financial markets has significantly reduced commission rates and profits (see Chapter 2) and may, as a consequence, increase the incidence of fraud. Deregulation has probably made fraud easier to perpetrate. Chapter 4 noted a low level of prosecutions. The abolition of exchange controls in Europe may well make fraud still more difficult to detect and prosecute.

Part B Financial Risks

2.6 Financial risks include operating risk (affected by the level of fixed costs and the volatility of revenues), financial gearing, and own-positions. The implications of these financial risks for

Table 6.1 Sources of market failure and alternative responses

Nature of risks (1)	Costs (2)	Sources of market failure (3)	Main responses to market failure (4)
A Fraud, theft, and non-contractual wealth transfers			
(i) without default	Uncompensated wealth transfers	Problem of: ● free rider ● lack of observability	Monitoring by IMRO
(ii) with default	Financial deficiency, disruption costs	Problem of: ● free rider ● information asymmetry leading to adverse selection	Monitoring by IMRO and insurance
B Financial risks and possibility of default			
(i) with separation of client balances	Disruption costs	Problem of: ● free rider ● incentives to engage in high-risk activities	Private audit Possible separation of positions

(ii) without separation of client balances	Disruption costs Clients' balance losses	*as above*	Monitoring by IMRO+insurance Possible separation of own-positions
C Risks in IM process (settlement, execution and counter party) (i) with default	Disruption costs Losses of clients' funds	Problem of: • free rider • incentives for IM firm to be slack in monitoring	Private audit+insurance for unfulfilled contractual obligations (or clients' funds entrusted to a custodian)

investors depend on whether client balances are separated from the IM firm's accounts.

2.7   Current IMRO rules require clients' balances to be kept in a separate bank account from that of the IM firm. IM firms that are licensed banks are exempt from this rule since they are subject to the supervisory function of the Bank of England.

2.8   The purposes of separating clients' cash balances are three-fold. First, in a liquidation, clients' balances do not contribute to settling other creditors' claims. Second, separation makes it more difficult for clients' funds to be used to meet the expenses of the firm. Finally, it may be easier to establish that misappropriation has taken place if funds are separated.

2.9   Separation does not necessarily mean that the IM firm ceases to have control over clients' balances. In a discretionary fund, clients' funds may still be moved at the IM firm's instigation with limited or no controls by a third party. As a result, misappropriation may still take place. Such risks could be much reduced if clients' balances were held by a custodian bank. Clients' balances that are controlled by a custodian bank will be described as 'strictly separated'.

2.10   Strict separation will also protect investors' funds that are in the process of transmission. Disposals or dividend payments are frequently credited to firms' accounts before being allocated to investors' accounts. In the process there is at least a temporary period of exposure. If there is strict separation, these funds will be credited directly to the custodian bank account.

2.11   If clients' balances are strictly separated, the only cost of default for investors is disruption. If there is separation, but not custodianship, the risk of loss from fraud remains. If clients' balances are not separated, then, in addition to disruption costs, default will in general impose losses on clients' balances.

2.12   Disruption will be minimized in circumstances in which the transfer of clients' accounts between IM firms can proceed unimpeded. This will be the case where (a) clients' funds and assets are clearly segregated from those of the firm and (b) the liabilities of IM firms can be readily settled. In that case, there should 'be no shortage of investment managers who are willing to absorb the clients of insolvent IM firms. The settling of claims may be more complex in circumstances in which IM firms take own-positions.

Part C   Risks in the IM Process

2.13   These include execution errors, settlement delays, and counterparty default. In the absence of fraud (included in Part 4), costs to investors arise only when there is default.

2.14   In that event, clients' assets may be lost. The loss of such assets may take place even if clients' balances are separated. For example, a major execution error, caused, say, by the negligence of the IM firm, may lead to default. As a result, the client may fail to receive the full proceeds or may be compelled to pay out larger sums than would have been the case in the absence of such errors. This can occur when a sale is made instead of a purchase and the delay in reversing the transaction takes place against a background of rising share prices. The default of the IM firm denies the client proper compensation. Chapter 3 noted that counterparty default presented the most serious threat. A counter-party default could impose losses of such magnitude as to threaten the solvency of IM firms.

2.15   To summarize, the primary risk that the investor faces is fraud. Where fraud results in default, the risk of uncompensated losses exists, and where default does not occur, fraud may not be fully revealed. The costs of financial distress are limited to disruption where clients' funds are strictly separated. Disruption costs are small if there is separation and IM firms do not take own-positions. Without separation, the potential losses from financial distress are much greater. Finally, the investor is at risk from the negligence of the IM firm in the execution and settlement of transactions and in selecting counterparties with whom to deal.

SECTION 3   The Sources of Market Failure

3.1   Column 3 of Table 6.1 relates the risks of the IM business to the sources of market failure.

3.2   Intervention by a regulatory authority is justified only in circumstances in which market failures can be identified. Market failures occur when prices and incentives do not fully reflect the costs and benefits of goods and services provided.

3.3   The most important class of market failures that arises in financial markets is imperfect information. Collection of information on the quality of firms and individuals within firms is a costly process. While individual investors have incentives to monitor (or to appoint agents to monitor), the incentives are inadequate. The benefits of any individual's monitoring accrue widely to all investors. As a consequence, individual investors hope to 'free-ride' on monitoring performed by others. For this reason, the amount of monitoring performed is below that amount required.

3.4   The free rider problem becomes more acute as the number of investors increases. It could be overcome by permitting managers of IM firms to appoint monitors, but the moral hazard problem is obvious in this case: poachers should hardly be permitted to choose the gamekeeper.

3.5   As a consequence, there will be inadequate information about the care taken by firms in executing and settling transactions, in assessing the quality of counterparties, and in evaluating the financial risks taken by firms and the likelihood of fraud being perpetrated. This class of market failure therefore afflicts all the risks described in this report.

3.6   IM firms may distinguish themselves from each other on the basis of superior investment performance. League tables of performance are regularly published, and successful firms advertise their positions in the tables. Unfortunately, such league tables may not be reliable either as efficient benchmarks of past performance or as good predictors of future performance. In the short run it is difficult to distinguish cases of superior performance from, say, luck. A number of academics have questioned the reliability of benchmarks that attempt to distinguish good or bad performances over any extended period.

3.7 A high-quality IM firm might try to distinguish itself in a number of different ways. For example, by using capital to signal to investors that there is little risk of default, the IM firm reduces incentives to pursue irregular dealings. Alternatively, an IM firm may merge with a larger group, both increasing the capital base and diversifying activities. This diversification may be in the IM field—more investment portfolios diversified across types of investors, securities, and countries. Diversification may also mean a portfolio of different financial institutions ranging from insurance to banking, thereby reducing the volatility of earnings fluctuations and the risk of default.

Part A   Fraud and Theft

3.8 Even in the absence of free-riding, it may be impossible or difficult to prevent fraud. There may be inadequate mechanisms for detecting fraud (observability problem), or difficulties in establishing that it has occurred (verifiability problem); and those involved in prosecuting against it may face considerable obstacles to proving fraud (enforceability problem). That enforceability is a real problem is evidenced by the low rate of prosecutions. The inexperience of jurors in complex fraud trials is felt to impede prosecution.

3.9 If a fraud or theft is detected, the firm will be compelled to compensate investors provided it has sufficient funds. In the event of inadequate funds, default will occur. If this happens, it can be reasonably assumed that the losses arising from previous frauds and thefts will be disclosed. There is no observability problem, at least *ex post*, in this case. However, insolvency usually implies that there are insufficient funds to compensate investors for losses suffered. This expectation of loss gives rise to an important information problem. If investors cannot determine the quality of IM firms prior to making their investments, then they will not be able to distinguish honest from dishonest firms. Since losses are expected (with some probability of fraud or theft), investors will attempt to recoup these losses by demanding higher returns from all IM firms, the honest as well as the dishonest. Since those higher returns are based on average expected loss rates, investors will tend to demand excessive returns from honest or high-quality firms. Honest firms may therefore be driven out of the market, giving rise to a deterioration in the average quality of firms. This problem is commonly referred to as *adverse selection*.

Part B   Financial Risks

3.10   The extent to which there are market failures associated with financial risks is closely related to the degree to which clients' funds are separated. In the absence of separation, there is an incentive for firms to undertake unduly risky activities, through for example holding own-investments. Since clients' funds are exposed to financial failure, the costs are borne by investors as well as by other creditors to the firm. Shareholders benefit from the gains of a high-risk strategy, but creditors and investors with funds at risk lose in the event of failure.

3.11   If investors anticipate that their funds are threatened by financial failure, they will demand higher returns. This will in turn force firms to seek higher returns, thereby exacerbating the moral hazard problem of firms choosing unduly risky activities.

3.12   In contrast, when clients' funds are separated, they are not exposed to the financial failure of the IM firm. As a consequence, the owners of IM firms do not benefit from increasing the riskiness of the firms' activities.

Part C   The Risks in the IM Process

3.13   A similar wealth transfer occurs in the presence of execution errors, settlement delays, and counterparty default. Here the gain to the IM firm is not financial but comes in the form of slack. Inadequate care taken by the IM firm in executing and settling transactions and choosing counterparties rebounds on the investor in the event of the firm being unable to pay full compensation. If the IM firm does not bear the costs of its actions, there will be a moral hazard risk of the IM firm taking inadequate care. This risk, unlike that of financial failure, is not removed by separation of clients' funds.

3.14 An important question that should be addressed is whether market failures described here are more widespread than in other industries, for example the car industry. There are at least three differences. First, problems of quality evaluation are more acute in the IM business. The absence of reliable benchmarks against which to measure performance undermines the ability of investors to establish quality at low cost. Thus, in the absence of default, fraud can go undetected and sloppy management systems can persist. Second, an IM firm provides a continuing service to a client, whereas after the sale of a car the car firm provides a service only when the warranty is invoked. This continuing service makes interruption of business a more serious concern in the IM industry than elsewhere. Third, and most substantially, by transacting in money, the risks of non-contractual wealth transfers are significantly greater in financial institutions than in other businesses. The risks are particularly great where IM firms hold cash balances. But even where they do not, the fact that investment businesses produce monetary returns means that expropriations may be particularly hard to detect.

3.15 To summarize, there are three classes of market failure that afflict the IM business and give rise to a prima facie case for regulation. The first is the free rider problem. This afflicts all the risks associated with the IM business described in Chapters 3 and 4. The second is the adverse selection risk of encouraging the entry of fraudulent firms and individuals into the IM business. In the absence of default, fraud may go undetected. In the presence of default, it will be inadequately compensated. In either event, there will be too much of it. The third class of market failure is the moral hazard problem of slack and high-risk investments held for the IM firm's account (referred to as 'own-positions').

SECTION 4   Market Failures Arising from Systemic Risks

4.1   The risks that have been considered to date differ in form from those that were described in the previous chapter for banks. The risks in this chapter have been firm-specific; those for banks were systemic, in particular the risk of runs. Some observers believe that systemic considerations may also apply to the IM business. According to one line of argument, securities markets might be significantly weakened by large-scale insolvencies in the IM industry. Gilts, equity, and other security prices might fall and the operation of markets be undermined.

4.2   The IM industry may be damaged by systemic risks because of the fee structure of firms. Since fee income and intangible value are usually proportional to market values of securities under management, any mispricing of market securities directly affects industry revenues. Mispricing of securities could occur as a result of excess volatility. Stock market prices, it is argued by some, are more volatile than fundamental values of the underlying assets of firms. This excess volatility creates particularly large fluctuations in the valuations of IM firms with their high beta coefficients, and increases the risk of financial collapse. If mispricing infects all firms, then falls in revenues will be industry-wide.

4.3   There is undoubtedly some force in these arguments. Chapter 3 reported the large element of fixed costs in running an IM business and noted that revenues of IM firms declined markedly after the 1987 crash. Even so, there were few instances of IM firms in distress because of the crash, despite the fact that share prices suffered their largest one-day decline in New York since 1914. This may merely reflect the financial reserves that IM firms had been able to accumulate after the long bull market. Were the crash to be repeated, one would be less confident about the ability of the IM industry to escape so lightly. However, there is little evidence to date of a serious risk of systemic collapse as a result of the fee structure of the IM business.

4.4 Of greater concern is the financial risk engendered by the own-positions of IM firms. Here industry risks are closer to those of broker/dealers than banks. In Table 6.2, the annualized volatility or standard deviation of the FTSE index is shown on a weekly basis before and after the crash of October 1987. Volatilities are calculated from options written on the index. It is apparent that volatility was about 20 per cent before the crash, but it more than trebled during the crash. In the weeks following the crash volatility gradually diminished, and by March 1988 it had returned to its pre-crash level.

4.5 In Table 6.3, the volatility forecasts implicit in option prices of varying maturities during the crash week are described. As at 23 October, the market's forecast (implicit in the prices of options maturing at end October) was 135 per cent for one week ahead. For five weeks ahead, the market's forecast of volatility was 78 per cent, and for 13 weeks it was 54 per cent. Although the crash week

Table 6.2 What happened to market equity risk around the time of the crash?

Week of	Implied annualized stand. dev. (%)
9 October 1987	20.7
16 October 1987	19.8
23 October 1987	69.8
30 October 1987	48.2
6 November 1987	42.7
13 November 1987	50.3
20 November 1987	49.1
March 1988	20.0

* Implied standard deviation of market is estimated from call options on FTSE index.

Table 6.3 Market forecasts of volatility at 23 October 1987

Implied standard deviation* for an option with maturity of:

1 week (October)	5 weeks (November	9 weeks (December)	13 weeks (January)
135%	78%	66%	54%

* Estimates taken from at-the-money FTSE options on 23 Oct. 1987. FTSE is an index of 100 equities, value-weighted. Implied volatilities calculated using Black–Scholes model.

was accompanied by a huge increase in market volatility, the forecasts suggest that such an increase was expected to be only temporary. By March 1988, market volatility had returned to its pre-crash levels.

4.6 The implication of these large changes in market volatility is that IM firms that hold substantial own-positions are subject to significant risks of financial failure. If systemic risks are thought to be important for the investment management industry, then the legal separation of own-positions of IM businesses should be considered.

4.7 However, there are two reasons why the regulatory authorities may not be too concerned about systemic risks. First, provided client balances are strictly separated, investors may not suffer direct losses in the event of failure. Moreover, the assets of failed IM firms should be marketable, provided that fraud has not been perpetrated. Disruption costs to investors should therefore be low.

4.8 Second, investment managers may perform a less crucial role in the operation of markets than broker/dealers. Many developed countries operate perfectly effectively without an extensive investment management industry. More likely, similar functions can be performed by a range of different institutional arrangements, but the demise of one would impose serious transitional problems.

4.9 If the authorities are concerned about systemic risks, then separation of own-positions from the legal entity that manages investor funds would substantially reduce the risks of failure and facilitate the transfer of assets of failed firms. Separation of own-positions would be more effective and less costly than imposing capital requirements.

SECTION 5   Correcting Market Failures

5.1 The market failures that were described in Section 3 had a common underlying cause: imperfect information on the part of investors. Inadequate information gave rise to adverse selection and moral hazard problems. This in turn reflected a tendency of a large number of small investors to free-ride, leading to an inadequate amount of monitoring.

5.2 To the extent that information collection and dissemination is efficiently pooled, this may be achieved by, for example, a credit rating agency. An appropriate solution may be thought to be the provision of information by a monitor or auditor.

5.3 Relying on the service of a monitor presents one serious difficulty: who is going to monitor the performance of the monitor? In some cases the answer is straightforward. If the quality of activities that are being monitored is eventually revealed, then so will the quality of the monitor. Provided that monitors can be penalized for bad services, the right incentives for monitors to perform their function properly will exist. Credit rating agencies illustrate this principle rather well. There is an acid test of the services provided by credit rating agencies, and that is the proportion of different classes of firms that go bankrupt. Credit rating agencies that do not have much predictive power are of little value and presumably are driven out of business.

5.4 There were three classes of risk described in the previous section for which quality was eventually revealed: fraud leading to financial default, financial risk, and risks in the investment management process leading to default. The monitoring of all three classes of risk is commonplace. Fraud and the quality of management systems are routinely monitored by auditors. Financial risks are evaluated by credit rating agencies.

5.5 The problem of inadequate incentives on monitors to perform their functions adequately can be overcome by requiring monitors to compensate for losses sustained by investors. If this is done and agreed in advance, the monitors will also be acting as insurers.

5.6 There is a serious impediment to the smooth operation of monitoring *plus* insurance. Insurance markets are undermined by the entry of fraudulent firms. Where fraud is a serious risk, insurance markets will not function effectively. In particular, the information required to establish the risk of fraud is unlikely to be available to a private firm. Access to central records will be required, together with extensive powers to prosecute on the basis of false information.

5.7 Fraud that does not result in default is not necessarily detected. It is a moot question whether incentives are any greater on public agencies than private firms to prosecute undisclosed fraud. The answer would appear to depend at least in part on the rules under which the public agency is operating.

5.8 To summarize, the market failures that were described in Section 3 arose from information problems. The first-best solution is therefore to seek ways of correcting the deficient provision of information. In the absence of fraud, private forms of monitoring should be available. Appropriate incentives can be imposed on monitors by combining insurance with monitoring. However, if there is a risk of fraud, the involvement of the public sector will be required to correct the adverse selection and observability problems that undermine the operation of the private insurance market.

5.9 Notice that capital is not an appropriate response to any of the individual firm risks. Either the risks are poorly correlated with financial performance—this is true of fraud and the risks in the IM process—or financial risks are not correlated across firms. Thus, capital is either a poor discriminator of firm quality or an expensive way of protecting investors.

5.10 This does not apply where risks are systemic in nature. The main source of systemic risk that was identified in Section 4 related to own-positions held by investment managers. Provided that own-positions are separated, the risks of simultaneous widespread failures in the IM business are small. Furthermore, if client balances are separated from those of the firm, the costs of failure are small. Thus, in marked contrast to banks and brokers/dealers, risks in the investment management business are not systemic in nature. The appropriate regulatory response is therefore also very different and, in particular, does not involve the imposition of capital requirements.

5.11. One of the implications of the observation that imperfect information is the underlying market failure is that, where there are a few large investors who are capable of monitoring the quality of IM firms for themselves, there is less justification for regulatory intervention. There may therefore be a case for making investor protection less onerous where IM firms have institutional rather than personal investors. For example, the requirement that insurance be provided might be relaxed for institutional investors. Indeed, it is difficult to see why institutions that are clients of IM firms should be distinguished from other creditors. This accords with a widely held belief that, in designing investor protection legislation, a distinction should be drawn between different classes of investor. However, since there are more extensive market failures associated with fraud than simply free-riding, regulation of fraud will still be required of public agencies by institutional investors.

SECTION 6   Alternative Forms of Investor Protection

6.1 Having set out the principles for correcting market failures, we now turn to a more detailed consideration of the merits and deficiencies of alternative responses. In this section we examine three different forms of investor protection: insurance, capital requirements, and monitoring/auditing. We distinguish between the private and public provision of insurance and monitoring/ auditing. In addition, we examine strict separation of clients' balances and own-positions.

6.2 In Table 6.4, the advantages and disadvantages of the first three are described. *Private insurance* pools capital but not information. It may be possible to achieve pooling without losing the advantages of competition by requiring private insurance firms to tender for the exclusive right to insure IM members. Tenders might be organized on a regular (say tri-annual) basis. Members of the Los Angeles Bar Association adopt this approach to purchasing an insurance policy against lawsuits.

6.3 Insurance is an incomplete form of protection. If default takes place, investors are protected against wealth transfers from fraud. However, if default does not take place and fraud or theft merely reduces investors' returns, no protection is afforded if losses are not detected. Furthermore, as discussed in Chapter 5, insurance markets are undermined by problems of adverse selection and moral hazard. Adverse selection means that insurers are unable to establish the quality of those seeking insurance and as a result set insurance rates on the basis of average quality. Inevitably, some firms succeed in gaining insurance on unduly favourable terms. Several forms of moral hazard may be present: (a) the insurer may fail to pay adequate compensation because of incomplete or inadequately specified insurance claims; (b) the insured may make unreasonable (or fraudulent) claims that are contractually unjustified; and (c) the insured may engage in excessively risky investments. Problems (b) and (c) are likely to be particularly serious and may result in honest and low-risk firms subsidizing dishonest and high-risk firms. In comparison, mutual insurance provides for both pooling of capital and information and protection against wealth transfers in the event of default. Again, there is no protection if fraud or other wealth transfers take place in the absence of default.

Table 6.4 Advantages and disadvantages of different forms of protection

| Form of protection | Pooling of capital | Pooling of information | Protecting investors from wealth transfers | | Costs |
			With default	Without default	
Private insurance	Yes	Limited	Yes	No	• Adverse selection • Moral hazard
Mutual insurance	Yes	Yes	Yes	No	• Limited pooling of risk • Adverse selection (more serious if firms are all insured) • Incentive problems
Capital	No	No	No	Partial	• Portfolio composition • Imperfect capital markets
Auditing and monitoring: Private	No	Limited	Partial	Partial	• Inadequate incentives
Public	No	Yes			

6.4   The costs of *mutual insurance* are similar to those of private insurance, with three important differences. First, the mutual insurance firm may be inadequately diversified because it is confined to one industry. This is likely to be an important deficiency in insuring against systemic risks that are correlated across firms. In California, firms that offer earthquake insurance policies are usually diversified. One solution would be for the mutual insurer to reinsure with other diversified insurers for losses in excess of a particular level. Second, adverse selection problems may be more severe if the mutual insurer finds it politically difficult to refuse insurance to low-quality IM firms. Thirdly, in the absence of competition, there may be inadequate incentives for mutual insurers to provide efficient and low-cost services. In the USA and the UK, we observe both private and mutual insurance.

6.5   *Capital requirements* do not achieve the benefits of the pooling of either capital or information. An example will illustrate. Suppose there are three IM firms of similar size and only one employee fraud will take place, but we are unaware which firm will default. The loss to investors will be £1 million. To prevent any fraud leading to default, capital requirements of £1 million must be imposed on each firm, totalling £3 million in aggregate. Thus, £3 of capital must be contributed for each £1 of investor's money at risk. In contrast, only £1 of capital need be held by an insurance company. There are, in addition, two distinct costs to capital requirements. First, if capital requirements are greater than those that the firm would normally choose, then the firm's portfolio of assets will be distorted. This will reduce the returns to investment management. Second, if capital markets are imperfect and additional equity is expensive, then the entry of new firms into the industry may be discouraged and the operation of small firms jeopardized. These problems will be discussed in greater detail in the next chapter.

6.6   *Capital* reduces risks of default by cushioning firms against financial loss. Capital therefore provides protection against risks that are related to the financial performance of the firm (see part II, 'Financial risks', of Table 6.1). *Capital requirements* are appropriate where firms do not take adequate account of the effect of their financial performance on that of other firms. They are therefore warranted where there are systemic risks that are related to the financial performance of firms. Where financial risks are highly correlated across firms, there are no savings from pooling risks. But capital provides no protection against fraud, irregular dealing, or negligence in the IM process. In contrast to banks and broker/dealers, there is therefore a very small role for capital in investor protection in the IM business. Only where own-positions are held might the imposition of capital requirements be justified.

6.7 A third form of protection is *screening and monitoring* of IM firms. Screening is the *ex ante* evaluation of the quality of individuals and firms prior to the commencement of operations; monitoring is the *ex post* assessment of the performance of firms once operations have begun. Screening is the function that regulators perform as part of their 'fit and proper' tests. It is also the activity that creditors undertake as part of the credit assessment process. It can therefore be undertaken by either public agencies or private firms, though the former may have access to information (such as police records) that is not publicly available.

6.8 Monitoring can also be performed by both regulators and private sector firms. The continuing surveillance of firms is a primary activity of regulatory agencies and private auditors. Regulators may be given greater powers of surveillance than private sector firms (for example, the ability to force disclosure of information) but may have fewer resources at their disposal. This is a feature of the US regulations described in Chapter 7, where the Securities and Exchange Commission (SEC) is able to inspect firms only on average on a five- to ten-year basis.

6.9 A crucial advantage of monitoring is that it has the potential of identifying fraud, theft, and non-contractual wealth transfers even when the IM firm has not defaulted. Also, financial systems as well as transactions can be examined. The firm may have to justify 'apparent' excessive trading in a portfolio. The US SEC requires the reporting of portfolio turnover and investigates turnover in excess of a pre-determined level.

6.10   A further advantage of monitoring is that, if it is combined with sufficiently tough penalties on individuals who abuse laws or rules, it can be limited to occasional surprise audits. In contrast, all potential new entrants have to be screened. Monitoring can therefore be a more effective and cost-efficient way of identifying fraud than screening. Difficulties arise, however, in circumstances in which adequate penalties cannot be imposed, even where fraud is identified. An important example of this is where fraudulent IM firms are outside the jurisdiction of the country in question and adequate reciprocity arrangements do not exist. This may be an important differences between the relatively domestic US IM business and the international UK industry.

6.11   A serious cost of auditing is that, unless the insurer is responsible for losses arising from inaccurate information, there are no financial incentives to audit to a high standard. In this respect, there are advantages to the insurer and auditor being one and the same party.

6.12   The fourth form of investor protection is *strict separation* of clients' balances and separation of own-positions. IMRO requires separation of clients' balances, with the exception of IM firms that are licensed banks. Notwithstanding separation, clients' funds may still be controlled by the IM firm. For example, when securities are purchased or sold, the IM firm may control temporarily the proceeds of sale or purchase. Even when funds are deposited in a client's account, a fraudulent IM manager may be able to misuse those funds. Strict separation could be obtained if clients' funds were placed with a custodian bank. In the USA, mutual funds frequently require all funds and securities to be held by custodian banks. In effect, strict separation is already imposed on the unit trust industry through the Trustee.

6.13   The advantages of strict separation can be seen in the light of a failure of a recent IM firm. In this particular case, the broker offset funds owed to clients' accounts managed by the IM firm against funds owed by the IM firm on purchases of securities on its own-account. Use of a third-party custodian would have rendered it much less likely that such an offset could have been effected unilaterally by a broker.

6.14 It has been suggested that the holding of own-positions can significantly increase the riskiness of IM firms. Separating own-positions from the pure IM activities will reduce the risks of default. If own-positions and clients' balances are separated, the risks of the IM business will be substantially diminished. IM firms would then be clearly distinguished from banks and broker/dealers on which capital requirements are appropriately imposed.

SECTION 7   Regulating the Investment Management Business

7.1 The previous sections have discussed four forms of investor protection: auditing/monitoring, capital requirements, insurance (both publicly and privately provided), and enforced separation of own-positions and client balances.

7.2 The following principles have been established.

(a) Monitoring with insurance is appropriate for most classes of risk.

(b) Public supply is justified only where there is a market failure in provision of private monitoring or insurance.

(c) This is true of fraud and theft where information on investment managers is a public good and criminal penalties should be available.

(d) The operation of private markets will be improved by the imposition of strict separation of clients' balances.

(e) Capital requirements should be employed only in circumstances in which risks are related to financial performance and are correlated across firms (i.e. systemic risks). Even then, we consider separation of own-positions to be a less costly and more effective remedy.

7.3 In column (4) of Table 6.1 the various responses to market failures are outlined. We consider each in turn.

Part A   Fraud and Theft

7.4 Monitoring by a public agency is required where there is a risk of fraud and theft. This arises from a market failure in the provision of private policing. In essence, the provision of policing by a public agency represents a subsidy to the entry of new firms that have not established a reputation by existing firms in the industry.

Part B   Financial Risks

7.5 The appropriate response to financial risks is a private audit, provided clients' balances are not at risk. This can be achieved by imposing strict separation on the IM firm. In this case the monitor can be appointed by the IM firm, since there is no question of fraud.

7.6 The costs of financial failure are limited to disruption. As was noted in the simulations in Chapter 3, the expected costs of disruption are low. The risks of financial loss can be further diminished by requiring own-positions to be separated from the investment management business. We believe this is appropriate if the costs of systemic risks are considered to be significant.

7.7 If client balances are not separated, then the response to the market failure is monitoring by a public agency and insurance. Public monitoring is preferred to private audit because of the costs to investors when investor balances may be lost. Insurance is required because the public agency will not detect all defaults prior to investor losses. Insurance is required to compensate investors when a default with a deficiency occurs. If the public agency offers the insurance, there are financial incentives to monitor to a high standard. However, in comparison with competitive private insurance, mutual insurance may be overpriced.

Part C   Risks in the IM Process

7.8   The appropriate response to settlement risk, execution errors, and counterparty default is private audit and compulsory insurance for any loss of clients' funds. The regulatory authority will wish to ensure that the form and scope of the audit and insurance arrangements are adequate.

7.9   Capital does not play an important role in investor protection. It is relevant only where investors' risk is negatively correlated with the profitability of the IM firm. In that case capital acts as a cushion. However, when risks and profitability are uncorrelated, capital cannot form an effective basis for investor protection. The relationship between risk and profitability is tenuous for several of the risks that have been described in this report. In particular, it is weak in the case of fraud. Indeed, some firms' high profitability may have been gained as a result of irregular dealings. We believe that, if all IM firms were ranked on the basis of disclosed profitability, it would be difficult to detect a correlation between the propensity to commit fraud, theft, and irregular dealings on the one hand, and profitability on the other. As a result, capital requirements cannot be a suitable form of protection.

7.10   Similarly, with execution errors, settlement risk, and counterparty risk, the relation between risks and profitability is weak. Only in the case of financial risks is the relation a strong one. But even here, the imposition of capital requirements is only justified by systemic risk considerations and is generally dominated by separation of own-positions. Otherwise, private monitoring and insurance is a more appropriate remedy, given the costs of requiring firms to hold capital.

7.11   If there is separation of clients' balances and own-positions, the IM firm will become a pure investment vehicle. This will result in much lower risks to investors. Losses, when they occur, will be smaller, and insurance will provide a final line of protection. IM firms may still leave the industry as a result of low profitability, but investors will not lose their funds; instead, other creditors will be at risk. It is not appropriate for the regulator to attempt to prevent exit from the industry. The maximum cost to investors will be some disruption until the management of funds is transferred to a new IM firm. Past evidence suggests that this process is relatively painless, assuming the absence of fraud. However, the regulatory agency may wish to ensure that, where exit or failure occurs, the reorganization process is efficient. This will be especially important where fraud has been perpetrated.

SECTION 8　Summary

8.1　This chapter has explained the nature of the market failures that give rise to a need for regulation. It has also considered the effectiveness of different regulatory responses in neutralizing market failures when private provision is unavailable.

8.2　The most important market failure in the IM business results from fraud, theft, and irregular dealing. Fraud creates adverse selection problems that necessitate the maintenance of public records and the imposition of criminal penalties. Investors may bear losses even in the absence of a firm's default. As a result detection is difficult, and the investor may not be compensated for losses sustained. The market failure associated with fraud justifies the involvement of a public agency.

8.3　Elsewhere, private remedies should be available. The main forms of investor protection that were recommended were monitoring and audit, insurance, and strict separation of client funds. If the costs of systemic risks are considered significant, separation of own-positions should be imposed. Regulatory requirements should be relaxed on IM firms with institutional investors.

8.4　The implementation of strict separation of client funds and own-positions would transform IM firms into pure investment vehicles. This would substantially diminish the risks borne by investors and would reduce the disruption costs of financial distress. The risks to investors that remained (associated with the IM process and running the business) could be eliminated by a combination of monitoring and insurance.

8.5 Capital requirements play virtually no role in the regulatory framework proposed in this chapter. The reason is that most risks bear only a tenuous relation to profitability.

8.6 Moreover, capital is not a particularly effective form of protection. Insurance has the advantage of pooling risks that are not highly correlated across firms, leading to much lower levels of capital across the industry as a whole. Only systemic financial risks justify the imposition of capital requirements. Even here, separation of own-positions is a less costly and more efficient alternative.

7 Capital Requirements in the UK and USA

SECTION 1 Introduction

1.1 The purpose of this chapter is to analyse the rules regarding capital that are currently required of investment managers in the UK.

1.2 Section 2 begins by describing the capital requirement rules of the relevant regulatory organization, the Investment Management Regulatory Organization (IMRO). Section 3 assesses the extent to which the rules provide the investor with protection against the risks described in Chapters 3 and 4 and the costs associated with each form of protection. It is argued that there are serious deficiencies, both in principle and practice, in the design of rules as currently formulated. Section 4 then considers how capital rules should be determined, assuming that capital is the preferred approach to investor protection. However, this assessment mainly reinforces the assertion made in the previous chapter that capital is not the appropriate form of protection for most of the risks that IMRO is seeking to neutralize. Section 5 describes regulation of IM firms by the Securities and Exchange Commission (SEC) in the USA. Section 6 summarizes the results of this chapter.

1.3 This chapter serves two purposes. First, it illustrates how the principles described in the previous chapter can be applied to a specific case, namely rules proposed by one British regulatory organization. Second, it forms the basis for our recommendations in the final chapter.

SECTION 2 The IMRO Rules on Capital Adequacy

2.1 In defining capital requirements, the IMRO rules distinguish between four classes of firms:

A   firms that do not execute transactions or have transactions executed by others for their clients (or themselves), i.e. firms that merely offer advice and do not hold clients' monies or assets;

B   firms that do execute transactions or have transactions executed for clients, but do not hold or control clients' monies or assets (or, if they do control clients' monies or assets, only make payments against receipt of titles to securities or release titles against receipt of money), i.e. managers that act as discretionary and non-discretionary agents and managers that act as principals but do not take counterparty risk;

C   firms that execute transactions or have transactions executed for clients and either hold or control (with counterparty risk) clients' monies or assets, i.e. advisers and managers that hold clients' monies or assets and managers that act as principals and take counterparty risk;

D   trustees of unit trusts.

2.2   The risks to investors are regarded as increasing progressively between classes A and C. Investors in class A firms are exposed to negligent and fraudulent advice and the disruption and inconvenience costs of interruption of business. Investors in class B firms are exposed to errors in executing transactions in addition to the risks of class A firms. In class C firms, losses can also arise from settlement delay, counterparty default, or custody of clients' monies or assets.

2.3   Class D firms are performing a special custodial function and are therefore subject to particular capital requirements.

2.4   Class A firms are only subject to an absolute minimum capital requirement of £5,000.

2.5   Class B firms are required to hold the *maximum* of:

(a)   an absolute minimum capital requirement of £5,000;

(b)   an expenditure-based requirement of 6/52 (i.e. 6 weeks' worth) of the firm's annual audited expenditure,[1]

(c)   a volume of business requirement of 0.1 per cent of the firm's previous quarter's gross value of transactions of purchases and sales of investments (not yet implemented).

2.6   Class C firms required to hold the *maximum* of:

(a)   an absolute minimum capital requirement of £5,000;

(b)   an expenditure based requirement of 13/52 (i.e. 3 months' worth) of the firm's annual audited expenditure;

(c)   a volume of business requirement of 0.3 per cent of the firm's previous quarter's gross value of transactions of purchases and sales of investments (not yet implemented).

2.7   Class D firms are required to hold an absolute minimum requirement of £4 million.

2.8   Capital is defined as

(a)   total assets excluding intangible assets less total liabilities excluding certain types of subordinated loans for companies that are subject to an absolute minimum capital requirement (this definition therefore applies to class A and D firms);

(b)   liquid assets for all other firms. Liquid assets are defined as for (a) but exclude tangible fixed asssets,[2] stocks,[3] fixed asset investments that cannot be readily sold, some classes of debtors, and a certain proportion of the market value of investments.[4] They include bank undertakings to make

---

[1] Expenditure excludes profit shares and bonuses paid to partners, directors, and employees and interest paid on clients' money, on the grounds that if there was a downturn in business then these items of expenditure could be reduced at little or no risk to the business. It also excludes commissions and fees that a firm pays on transactions on behalf of other parties.

[2] Properties purchased with mortgages can be included up to the value of the mortgage or 85% of the value of the property, whichever is the lower.

[3] Unless they are stocks of investments held for trading purposes, in which case the position risk adjustment described under investments applies.

[4] Floating rate investments are valued at 95% of their market value, fixed rate investments and deposits that are not encashable within 90 days at 90%, investments in stocks listed in the FT Actuaries World Index at 80%, and

payments up to a specified amount (which cannot exceed the excess of a firm's capital requirement over 6/52 of its expenditure requirement) on specified terms in the event of a firm being in default.[5]

2.9 The inclusion of an absolute minimum capital requirement was justified on the grounds of credibility, good faith, financial integrity, and the fact that there are unavoidable start-up costs of purchasing essential fixed assets, paying membership subscriptions, and taking out insurance cover (which is now obligatory). The figure of £5,000 was arrived at as follows:

Membership subscriptions	£2,000
Insurance cover	£1,000
Fixed assets	£1,000
Telephone, stationery	£1,000

2.10   The inclusion of an expenditure requirement reflects an attempt to protect against the disruption and inconvenience associated with interruption to a class B business and the direct costs (to clients' monies or assets) that investors in class C firms incur in the event of a cessation of business. It was felt that a business should hold sufficient capital to meet periods of loss of income and if necessary the orderly running down of a business, i.e. the operating risks described in Chapter 3. Six weeks' expenditure was thought appropriate in circumstances in which costs to investors were limited to disruption and inconvenience (i.e. class B firms); three months' expenditure was felt necessary in other circumstances (class C firms).

investments listed on recognized exchanges at 70%. Other investments are valued at 50% of the lower of their cost and valuation. Unit trust managers' positions in boxes are valued at 97% of the bid value of units in fixed or floating rate securities, 95% of the bid value of units in US, Canada, or Japanese equities, 94% of the bid value of units in European (including UK) equities, and 90% of the bid value of units in other equities.

[5] The limitation on bank undertakings has the effect of requiring firms to hold capital amounting to 6 weeks' worth of expenditure in a form other than bank undertakings.

2.11 Inclusion of a volume of business requirement was justified on the basis of the risks arising from the investment management process (in particular, execution errors and counterparty default). The accumulation of transactions over the previous quarter was regarded as a suitable compromise between the need for timely information and the smoothing of random fluctuations. A level of 0.1 per cent of the gross value of bargains was thought appropriate in circumstances in which firms do not have custody of clients' monies or assets, or to avoid counterparty risk through matching exchanges of securities and money. A level of 0.3 per cent was felt to be required in other cases. A ratio of 0.1:0.3 was chosen to maintain the same ratio of four and twelve weeks' expenditure in Securities and Investments Board (SIB) rules.

2.12 A gross (liquid and illiquid) definition of capital was thought appropriate in circumstances in which an investor had limited financial exposure to a business, i.e. class A firms, which only provide investment advice and do not handle clients' monies or assets. In other cases a more stringent liquid capital requirement was felt to be necessary. The discounts on the market value of investments in the definition of liquid capital are position risk adjustments.

2.13 The determination of capital requirements for different classes of firms is summarized in Table 7.1.

2.14 There are several points that should be emphasized about the reasoning that lay behind IMRO's capital adequacy rules.

(a) Capital requirements were seen to be justified by operating risks (i.e. risks of disruption to the business) and risks in the investment management process (i.e. execution errors and counterparty problems).

(b) Capital requirements (beyond minimum requirements) *per se* were not justified by negligence, fraud, and misappropriation of clients' assets. Establishing a capital requirement to protect against these risks did not seem to be feasible.

(c) Position risks are reflected in the valuation of eligible assets, not capital requirements.

Table 7.1 The Basis of existing IMRO capital adequacy rules

Nature of IM business	Classification of firm	Risk to investor	Capital requirements proposal	Eligible capital
Advisers not holding clients' money or assets	Class A	Negligence, fraud, disruption	Minimum absolute	Liquid plus illiquid assets
Managers acting as (non-discretionary or discretionary) agents not holding clients' money or assets	Class B	Negligence, fraud, disruption, execution error	Minimum absolute, 6 weeks' expenditure and 0.1% of volume	Liquid assets
Managers acting as principals not taking counterparty risk and not holding clients' money or assets				
Managers acting as principals taking counterparty risk	Class C	Negligence, fraud, disruption, execution error, counterparty risk, loss of clients' monies or assets	Minimum absolute, 3 months' expenditure and 0.3% volume	Liquid assets
Advisers and managers holding clients' money or assets				

SECTION 3   An Evaluation of the IMRO Capital Adequacy Rules

3.1   The previous chapter discussed the case for regulation of the investment management business. It described the market failures that may give rise to the need for regulation. Failure to provide adequate protection will have both efficiency and distributional costs. Investors will be discouraged from using the services of investment managers if there are risks that losses may be inflicted by the investment manager and if those risks are difficult to evaluate. A certain level of regulation may thus benefit both investor and the investment management industry by reducing variability in quality where the quality of the services cannot be readily established.

3.2   Furthermore, the wealth transfers arising from fraud, negligence, and financial failure may be deemed to be unacceptable even if they do not interfere with the investment process. Losses may be large in relation to the total wealth of those affected and may be incurred by those who are thought to be least able to absorb them. Fraud, as a form of theft, clearly cannot be countenanced at any time. The ease with which it can be perpetrated and the scale on which it can occur in the financial management business make fraud an obvious reason for regulating the financial services industry.

3.3   On the other hand, regulation imposes costs on firms that are regulated and in many cases on their clients. Capital requirements interfere with firms' portfolio allocations and impose costs of raising capital in the presence of imperfect capital markets, in particular on small firms. Larger firms may choose inefficient corporate organizations to meet capital requirements, may be discouraged from undertaking certain types of activities, and may prefer to locate their operations in other financial centres. Smaller firms may find the costs of entering the financial management business unduly onerous, may be driven out, or may have their growth constrained by capital requirements.

3.4 A regulatory arrangement that provides inadequate investor protection will be described as being afflicted by *type I* error and unjustified costs of regulation will be said to give rise to *type II* errors. In designing a regulatory system, one is seeking to minimize both types of errors. In general, both types of errors will be encountered and there will have to be a trade-off between the two.

3.5 Subsequent paragraphs will evaluate the errors associated with current IMRO capital adequacy rules. It is, however, worth noting at this point that there is a striking mirror image between the circumstances that give rise to market failures and provide some justification for capital requirements, and the reasoning behind the IMRO rules, as summarized in paragraph 2.14. Here, capital requirements were thought to be justified by risks in the investment management process and operating risks. In neither case does an obvious market failure arise. Where market failures quite clearly are likely to arise, as in the case of fraud and the holding of clients' balances, capital requirements were thought to be an inappropriate response.

3.6 The analysis of IMRO rules begins by abstracting from a detailed discussion of their precise formulation; instead, it assesses whether the approach of using the greater of an operating risk and a volume of business measure is valid in principle. Table 7.2 summarizes the prevalence of type I and type II errors created by this form of capital requirement for three classes of risk: fraud (including employee fraud against the firm, companies set up to defraud, and companies that were induced into fraud by financial distress); risks associated with the investment process (execution errors, settlement delay, and counterparty risk); and risks in operating the business. The classes of risk are categorized by size of firm.

3.7 In Chapter 4, fraud was noted to be a particularly serious problem in comparatively young companies with little financial history. If small companies have low levels of expenditure and low volumes of business, then both expenditure and volume

Table 7.2 Frequency of type I and type II errors in using expenditure-based and volume-of-business capital requirements as protection against three types of risk*

| Risk | Expenditure requirement | | | | Volume-of-business requirement | | | |
| | Small firms | | Large firms | | Small firms | | Large firms | |
	Type I errors (i)	Type II errors (ii)	Type I errors (iii)	Type II errors (iv)	Type I errors (v)	Type II errors (vi)	Type I errors (vii)	Type II errors (viii)
(1) Fraud	High	Low	Low	High	High	Low	Low	High
(2) The investment process	Medium	High	Medium	High	Medium	Medium	Medium	Medium
(3) Risks in operating the business	Medium	Medium	Medium	Medium	Medium	High	Medium	High

* Type I error: implies inadequate protection; type II error: implies excessive capital.

requirements will be low. They will therefore provide little protection against fraud; i.e., there will be a high incidence of type I errors (line (1), cols. (i) and (v)). If large firms have high levels of expenditure and volumes of business they will have large and for the most part excessive capital requirements, thereby creating a low incidence of type I errors (line (1), col. (iii) and (vii)) but a high incidence of type II errors (line (1), cols. (iv) and (viii)).

3.8 In evaluating the success of capital requirements in correcting risks in the investment process and risks in operating the business, it has to be borne in mind that IMRO's rules impose *the larger of expenditure and volume requirements*. Risks in the investment process may relate to a firm's volume of business. Thus, volume-of-business rules may limit risks in the investment process (line (2), cols. (v)–(viii)). But risks in the investment process are not directly related to firms' expenditure. For firms with levels of expenditure that are large in relation to their volume of business (for example those managing assets of private clients), the expenditure requirement will bite and thus impose too high a capital requirement; i.e., type II errors will be high for both small and large firms (line (2), cols. (ii) and (iv)).

3.9 Operating risks may relate to firm's expenditures. Thus, expenditure requirements may limit operating risks (line (3), cols. (i)–(iv)). But these risks are not directly related to volumes of business. For firms with large volumes of business on a small expenditure base (for example large discretionary trusts and pension funds), the volume-of-business requirement will bite and thus impose too high a capital requirement; i.e., type II errors will be high for both small and large firms (line (3), cols. (vi) and (viii)).

3.10 To summarize, Table 7.2 suggests that type II errors (i.e. excessive capital) are particularly serious problems in large firms. If fraud is the main risk in small firms, then type I errors (inadequate protection) are of primary concern. Furthermore, the discriminatory power of both expenditure and volume-of-business requirements is very limited. For example, the risks associated with the investment management process are dependent on the quality of systems employed, the parties with whom a firm transacts, the types of markets in which a firm transacts, and the settlement systems that are employed. These cannot be accurately captured by a crude volume-of-business measure. Correspondingly, the risk of financial failure is a function of the services that a firm provides, the reputation that a firm has established, and the contractual basis on which individuals are employed. Again, none of these is captured by the expenditure requirement. Type I and II errors are therefore described somewhat generously as being of 'medium frequency'.

3.11 Closer scrutiny of the rules reveals problems in their detail as well as their design. Section 2 of Chapter 6 described the relative magnitudes of different classes of risks. It noted that, if the only risk that arises is that of default, then disruption and inconvenience costs are probably comparatively small. The major costs come from investment managers holding clients' assets. The simulations in Chapter 3 showed that costs borne by investors rise rapidly with the value of clients' assets held, so that capital requirements should be related to amounts at risk (i.e. assets held by the investment manager) as well as the determinants of the risks.

3.12 Second, the discussion of the risks in Chapter 3 and the results of the questionnaire suggest that there is considerable variation in the way in which losses associated with the investment management process are distributed between investor and firm. In determining the size of capital requirements to be imposed on firms, account has to be taken of the terms on which the investment manager is employed by the investor. Currently, a distinction is drawn between managers who initiate transactions and those who do not. The allocation of losses associated with, for example, settlement risk is clearly more complex than this distinction would suggest.

3.13 Third, Chapter 3 and the questionnaire recorded several influences on the risks associated with the investment management process: the markets in which firms transact, the securities in which they transact, the parties with whom they transact, and the extent to which activities are subcontracted. The questionnaire suggested that at least some information is now available on the relevance of these characteristics to the determination of capital requirements.

3.14 Fourth, no account is currently being taken of the intangible valuation and the risk of firms. The capital requirements of three firms, each with annual expenditures of £1 million but one with revenues of consistently around £1 million, one with revenues that average £1 million but fluctuate between zero and £2 million, and one with negligible revenues, are all the same! This is clearly undesirable and suggests an important weakness in the current design of the rules.

3.15 Fifth, IMRO's treatment of position risk is not consistent with either the approaches of other regulatory organizations or IMRO's treatment of other risks in the investment management business. Instead of increasing capital requirement, discounts are applied to the valuation of assets that are subject to position risks. While there is a relation between the two, correlations in returns across assets and between own-positions and other risks make that relation complex and nonlinear. Furthermore, no account is being taken of the portfolio considerations that have played a central role in the formulation of capital requirements for market-makers.

3.16 Sixth, for the most part, only liquid capital can be counted towards a firm's capital requirements. It is important to distinguish between capital that is supposed to diminish risks of insolvency, capital that is supposed to reduce losses in the event of insolvency, and capital that is designed to meet the immediate requirements of the firm. The first is the ongoing net worth of the firm and includes intangible valuations; the second is the disposal valuation; and the third is working capital. The third comes closest to the IMRO definition of capital. It is relevant to circumstances in which liquidity is a prime consideration of investors. It is applicable to bank capital requirements. It is also relevant to other financial institutions where investors suffer severe disruption costs from temporary interruptions to business. It is not relevant to protecting investors against losses sustained as a result of incompetence or errors on the part of investment managers.

3.17 A liquid capital requirement may therefore be sought of IM firms that could be faced with disruption owing to insufficient liquid reserves while still solvent. This requirement does, however, have to be clearly distinguished from one designed to protect against direct liabilities arising from errors in the investment management process. This distinction is not currently being made.

3.18 Were the principles underlying the current formulation of IMRO's rules to be accepted, then their design would have to be radically altered. Much more account would have to be taken of the risks borne by individual firms as determined by their contractual relation with investors and the nature of the transactions that they perform. Capital requirements would have to be more directly related to the potential losses that investors can sustain. More attention would have to be given to the definition of capital, and the position risk requirements would have to be reformulated. But most important of all, a more systematic approach to the design of capital rules would be sought, which achieved consistency in treatment of different classes of risks and correctly accounted for the interrelation between risks.

SECTION 4   A Framework for the Determination of Optimal Capital Requirements

4.1 To understand how such an approach can be developed, it is necessary to go back to a basic description of the investment management business. Figure 7.1 characterizes one aspect of the problem that the regulator faces. His job is to limit the losses that can be sustained by the investor on account of failures in the investment management. One influence on the exposure of investors is the risk that the investment manager may encounter financial difficulties. The regulator monitors periodically. Between monitoring periods the firm incurs costs of operating the business and sustains losses from failures in the investment process; the services that the investment manager performs generate income in the form of fees and commissions; and there are profits or losses on the firm's own-positions. The question that the regulator wishes to answer is, given information from the firm's current accounts, in particular the valuation of its assets and liabilities, what is the probability that the firm will have encountered financial difficulty by the next monitoring period? The answer to this question is clearly dependent on the expected level of earnings and expenses of the firm from management activities and own-positions, the distribution of these earnings and costs about their mean, *and* their correlation. Given information about opening balance sheets, expected returns on own- and intangible capital, and the variances and covariances in these returns, a probability of financial distress can be determined.

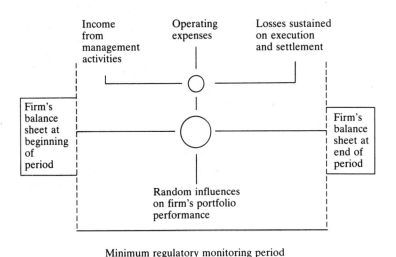

Minimum regulatory monitoring period

Fig. 7.1 The conceptual framework

4.2 Those risks are applied to the possible losses that investors can sustain to derive the expected value of the loss to the investor associated with the investment management process (as distinct from the risk inherent in the investors' assets themselves). There were three classes of risk discussed in Chapter 3: (a) disruption and inconvenience costs of interruption to business, (b) losses sustained by clients' assets and monies, and (c) the direct costs to investors of errors in execution, settlement delays, and counterparty default which the firm is unable to compensate. As the simulation analyses demonstrated, some of the expected costs are simply products between expectations and possible losses (e.g. disruption costs); others are more complex interactions between probabilities and the exposure of investors (clients' balances and the direct costs of the investment management process). Having determined the expected value of the potential loss to the investor for a given opening balance sheet, the required opening level of capital to reduce this expected value to an acceptable level can be determined. The acceptable level is a political decision, reflecting a trade-off between the type I errors referred to above of protecting investors against losses and the type II errors of interfering in the investment management process. The greater the emphasis on minimizing the probabilities of substantial losses sustained by a few investors, the greater the capital requirement that will be sought. The greater the emphasis on cost reductions in the investment management industry, the smaller will be capital requirements. Figure 7.2 characterizes the determination of the optimal level of capital.

4.3 An interesting implication of this approach is that capital requirements are inversely related to periods between monitoring. This serves to emphasize the fact that monitoring and capital requirements are *substitutes* for firms of particular risk characteristics. Capital was a response to imperfect information. To the extent that information can be improved through monitoring, capital requirements diminish. However, looking across firms of different risk characteristics, increased capital *and* monitoring may be required of riskier firms.

Costs to clients arising from:

(A) Default   Disruption and inconvenience

Non-separation of clients' money and assets

(B) Direct costs borne by clients from execution errors, settlement delays, counterparty default, and custody problems

Probability and cost of default determine the average estimated cost

Requirement that average estimated cost $<X\%$

$\implies$ Probability of default $<Y\%$

$\implies$ Capital requirement $>Z\%$

Fig. 7.2   How capital requirements are determined

4.4   An important feature of this approach is that it is applicable to the determination of capital for any type of financial institution. It is quite consistent with the Securities and Investments Board's capital requirements for brokers and dealers. This relates the capital requirement on a particular security to estimates of the contribution of the risk of that security to the risk of a firm's portfolio. All that this analysis does is to include operating risks and risks of the investment management process in the set of total risks.

4.5   To implement this procedure, the risks associated with the operation of an investment manager and the investment management process have to be determined. The risks were discussed at length in Chapter 3. Operating risks were described as being a function of market prices, aggregate savings patterns, and the proportion of fixed costs in the IM business. These risks are dependent on the volatility of security prices, the types of transactions performed (e.g. the distribution between domestic and overseas markets, gilts and equities, and discretionary and non-discretionary services), and the contractual basis on which the investment manager is employed.

4.6 Some guidance on the magnitude of these risks was provided by the volatility of security prices, measures of gearing, and the questionnaire on the risks in the investment management business. Case histories of financial distress and fraud provided evidence on past losses. But one of the difficulties that the regulator (and the private insurer) faces in attempting to set capital requirements and insurance premiums is that there is little experience of previous losses. The precision with which risks can be established is very limited. Furthermore, the relation between firm characteristics and capital requirements is complex. The expected value of potential losses sustained by clients is related to the value of client balances and the risks associated with the investment management process in a nonlinear fashion. Correlations between different types of risks (e.g., the relation between execution errors and firm performance was mentioned in Chapter 3) introduce further nonlinearities.

4.7 Of course, it is possible to make simplifications. Firms could be categorized into risk classes along the lines of the classifications that were used in explaining the existing rules. The analysis of risks in Chapter 3 suggests that the primary questions in establishing risk classes are: (a) Does the firm provide management as well as advisory services? (b) Does it hold or control clients' monies or assets even for a short period? (c) Does it take on settlement and counterparty risk? (d) Does it operate in overseas markets? (e) Does it transact in equity as well as gilt markets? (f) Does it take on own-positions? Risks increase as firms answer yes to more of these questions. But the fewer the risk classes, the greater the inaccuracy in the simplification. Furthermore, within risk classes, nonlinear rules relating capital to products of monies held and risks will be required.

4.8 It is thus clear that, in addition to there being objections to both the principles and the precise specification of the IMRO rules, there are serious difficulties involved in implementing any set of capital adequacy rules that does justice to the underlying relation between capital and investor protection. All of this would have been quite powerful ammunition for critics of current capital adequacy rules were it not for the fact that there is a still more fundamental objection: capital is not in general the preferred form of investor protection.

4.9 The current system of regulating the investment management business has emerged as a response to two sets of questions: the scale of risks involved in the investment management business, and the extent to which those risks can be measured. Capital has been proposed as a form of investor protection in circumstances in which risks were thought to be appreciable and, at least to a degree, measurable. For example, expenditure and volume of business were selected as capital requirements for reasons of ease and reliability of measurement. This approach to selecting capital requirements is flawed.

4.10 The first question that should be asked is where, if anywhere, do market failures arise that require public intervention. Capital requirements have focused on operating risks and the risks of the investment management process. But as mentioned in the previous chapter, these are not the areas in which market failures are most likely to arise. Random influences on performance are diversifiable risks that the private sector can absorb. On the other hand, there are market failures associated with fraud and the holding of clients' balances that justify public intervention. The analysis of type I and II errors in Table 7.1 suggests that existing capital requirements are particularly deficient in protecting against fraud.

4.11 As a way of providing protection against random disturbances that are uncorrelated across firms, capital requirements are very inefficient. By imposing requirements at the level of individual firms, the total capital being demanded of the investment management business is well in excess of that needed to protect the industry as a whole.

4.12 To the extent that performance is not random and is related to, for example, the quality of a firm's management system, detailed monitoring is required. A case for investor protection was made on the basis of imperfect information about the quality of firms. In the absence of regulation, clients' investments may be exposed to an excessive risk of failure simply because there is deficient monitoring of the quality of IM firms. Compulsory insurance of those funds can therefore be justified. In providing that insurance, the private sector may impose capital requirements on firms for screening and moral hazard reasons. Those requirements will probably be set on the basis of a risk classification scheme described earlier and loss experiences. The role of the public sector is then limited to improving the operation of private insurance markets through the provision of monitoring and disciplining which is unavailable to the private sector. Policing and criminal prosecution are two instruments that are available to the public but not the private sector, and they are appropriately employed in cases of fraud. This is where the comparative advantage of the public sector lies.

4.13 It is also incorrect to regard private sector insurance as a supplement to capital rules set by a regulatory organization. As noted above, existing rules allow firms under certain circumstances to count bank guarantees towards liquid capital requirements. Capital requirements are therefore being treated as the correct base from which deductions can be made for contributions from the private sector. As the framework of analysis in this chapter has demonstrated, the relation between investor protection and capital requirements is complex and cannot be captured by existing rules. The starting point should be that a certain level of *investor protection* should be provided in, for example, the form of insurance. To the extent that the private sector is unable to provide this, resort will have to be made to public monitoring and mutual insurance.

4.14 The abolition of capital requirement may be thought to weaken the control that regulators can exert over high-risk IM firms. The violation of a capital requirement rule may be used not necessarily to elicit penalties but rather to provide a justification for intensified monitoring. Bond covenants serve similar purposes in transactions between borrowers and lenders. But capital

8 Summary and Conclusions

SECTION 1   Introduction

1.1   This report has examined the role of capital requirements in investor protection.

1.2   The task that we were set was to establish whether capital requirements are an appropriate form of investor protection, and whether the amounts that IMRO has required of its members are correct. In undertaking this analysis, it has been neccssary to evaluate capital requirements in relation to other forms of investor protection.

1.3   The report described the investment management business in the UK, the function that investment managers perform, and the risks to which those functions give rise. It then posed the question: What are the market failures that create a need for investor protection, and what are the appropriate ways in which that protection should be provided? In the process of answering this question, we found it necessary to identify how investment management is distinguished from other industries and why a particular need for regulation arises in this but not other sectors of the economy.

1.4   In writing this report, we have become acutely aware of a problem that confronts the designer of a regulatory system. The protection of the investor provokes similar sentiments to those that are encountered in discussions about health care and support for the poor. The personal investor is perceived to be vulnerable to the skills and ambitions of the professional investment manager. In large part, this reflects a public fear of fraud. But its manifestation goes beyond mere prevention of fraud.

1.5 The Financial Services Act states that those providing financial services should be seen to be 'fit and proper'. It refers to 'the orderly running down' of businesses. These are proper and worthy sentiments. But the risk they create is that, in interpreting them, the regulator may regard his role as extending beyond the provision of investor protection to the administration of the industry and individual businesses. On this basis we might wish to regulate building contractors, who enter and leave the industry with great regularity, and who frequently impose significant cost and inconvenience on clients when exiting. Therefore the requirement that capital be held so as to discourage exit could be widely applied. Equally, it is easy to assert that a necessary part of the proper running of a business is the holding of capital. Of course it is. But that is not the same as saying that it is the role of the regulator to *require* a business to hold capital. As we have been at pains to note in Chapter 5, firms hold capital of their own accord as a normal part of running a business. In most industries the government does not see its function as being one of dictating a minimum level of capital that firms should hold. *It is only where the level of capital that firms decide to hold is less than the amount that society might legitimately wish them to hold that a prima facie case for regulation emerges.*

1.6 There are three stages to an evaluation of current regulatory requirements. The first is to identify possible market failures. The second is to determine the scale and significance of risks that can create market failures. The third is to establish the best way of correcting these market failures and to compare existing and proposed requirements. Section 2 considers the two classes of market failure that can occur in an investment business—systemic risks and asymmetric information. Section 3 describes the scale and significance of these risks. They are discussed under the four headings used in this report: fraud and theft, financial failure, risks arising in the investment management process, and systemic risks. Section 4 compares IMRO's response to these four classes of risk with that of the report. Section 5 sets out the costs and benefits of the proposed changes. It does not attempt a quantitative cost–benefit analysis, but suggests that a prima facie case for change has been established in this report.

SECTION 2　Market Failures and Investor Protection

2.1　Regulation of financial institutions is most commonly associated with banks. There are two reasons for this. First, banks play a central role in economic activity, and widespread bank failures can have unacceptable repercussions elsewhere. Second, the failure of one bank can undermine the operation of another. The mismatch between maturities of banks' assets and liabilities makes them vulnerable to risks of 'runs'. A run may be prompted by a real deterioration in the underlying financial position of a bank; alternatively, it may merely reflect a perceived risk that other investors may withdraw their deposits prematurely. Such concerns among investors may stem from failures elsewhere in the banking system. In other words, banks' performances are intimately interrelated, if only for reasons of reputation. Widespread failures have serious repercussions elsewhere in the economy. Together, these observations imply that there are *systemic risks* in the banking sector.

2.2　Banks are not the only financial institutions where systemic risks arise. Brokers and dealers perform a central function in the operation of a securities market. They enhance liquidity and accelerate the execution of transactions. Whether this function is of broader economic significance outside the financial sector depends on the wider relevance of securities markets to economic activity. The role of securities markets differs appreciably between countries.

2.3　As is the case with banks, there are significant interlinkages between brokers and dealers. Since both brokers and dealers take investment positions on their own account ('own-positions'), their solvency is threatened by financial failures elsewhere in the system. These interlinkages create risks of market-wide failures which threaten economic stability in security-market-based economies.

2.4　Whether systemic risks are present in investment management thus revolves around two issues: (a) the extent to which the performance of investment managers is affected by that of other financial institutions, and (b) the wider consequence of financial failure in investment management.

2.5 Provided that investment managers do not take positions on their own account, interlinkages between firms are limited. Although the financial performances of investment managers are closely correlated (through, for example, fee income), their exposure to the solvency of others stems largely from the investment positions that they take on their own account.

2.6 Furthermore, if investment managers do not hold clients' balances, the consequences of financial failure for investors are limited to disruption of business (in the absence of fraud). Provided that there are no serious impediments to the transfer of invested funds of failed businesses to new management, those disruption costs are small. In sum, unlike other parts of the financial sector, *there is little evidence of market failure arising from systemic risk in investment management.*

2.7 The second class of market failure results from *imperfect information*. Where the clientele of an investment manager is widely dispersed, there may be inadequate incentives for individual investors to evaluate the quality of firms. As a consequence, high-quality firms will not be adequately distinguished from low-quality firms, and investors will require excessively large returns of high-quality firms and inadequate returns of low-quality firms. Therefore, there will be inappropriate pricing of risks. Market failures will be particularly pronounced where IM firms have individual rather than institutional clients. In general, institutions will have more resources and be better equipped to undertake monitoring than individuals. *Less regulation may therefore be required of IM firms serving institutional rather than individual clients.*

2.8 In the presence of imperfect information, investors are exposed to three classes of risks: (a) fraud, theft, and irregular dealing; (b) financial failure; and (c) risks arising in the investment management process (execution and settlement).

2.9 Market failures associated with fraud, theft, and irregular dealing are particularly serious. In the absence of financial failure, they are difficult to detect. In the presence of financial failure, adequate resources to compensate investors for losses sustained are not in general available. Therefore fraud, theft, and irregular dealing either remain undetected or are at best only partially corrected.

2.10 Negligence or incompetence in the investment management process can also create non-contractual wealth transfers. If default occurs, then adequate resources will not in general be available to compensate investors fully. If default does not occur, then, provided that there is no attempt to disguise errors, investors will usually be compensated. Thus, only those failures in the investment management process that result in insolvency are potential sources of market failure.

2.11 In the absence of fraud, theft, negligence, or incompetence, financial failure imposes two forms of loss on investors. The first results when investor funds that are not separated from those of the investment 'business' become part of the pool of assets available to meet creditors' claims in the event of insolvency. The second reflects the disruption costs imposed on investors by the termination of business. Where all clients' funds (including those in transition between investments) are separated, only disruption costs occur.

2.12 The implication of this is that, *where client funds are separated, market failures are restricted to those resulting from dishonesty, incompetence, and negligence. Pure financial failure is of limited significance.* In contrast to other financial institutions, where systemic risks arising from financial failure are the primary cause of market failure, investment management is most prone to distortions created by imperfect information about the integrity and ability of individuals. *This distinction suggests that the appropriate form of regulation of investment businesses may be very different from that of other financial institutions.*

SECTION 3 The Risks of Investment Management

3.1 Establishing the scale and significance of risks in investment management is not straightforward. Some information is available from published data but, as Chapters 3 and 4 record, considerable reliance has had to be placed on surveys and interviews. While we received a great deal of co-operation from people involved in the operation and regulation of investment businesses, it has been possible to gain only a general impression of the scope and scale of risks. The fact that risks are difficult to quantify with precision makes regulatory arrangements that rely on precise estimates particularly unreliable. Chapter 7 argued that capital requirements fall into this category.

3.2 A quite consistent picture of the scale of risks in investment businesses emerged from the interviews and survey.

Part A Fraud and Theft

3.3 If fraud is hard to detect without the failure of the IM firm, so is irregular dealing. For example, some concern was expressed in interviews that purchases of units from the trustee (by the manager of the unit trust) were sometimes made at prices ruling prior to the purchase date—referred to as 'backpricing'. Some IM managers felt strongly that the trustee's role could be tightened in this regard. However, trustees interviewed denied there was a serious problem. Changes to pricing rules should diminish some of these excesses.

3.4 Companies that have been set up to defraud have a number of distinctive characteristics. They have had low levels of initial capital, have operated for short periods, have employed hard selling techniques, have taken investment positions on their own account, and have not strictly separated clients' bank accounts from those of the firm.

3.5 There are a number of cases of an IM firm being a member of a larger group and thereby being affected by the financial difficulties of the group. This was particularly in evidence during the secondary banking crisis and property price collapse in the 1970s. Other IM firms that ran into financial problems often took significant position-risks or invested in connected firms. Financial problems in unit trusts have arisen from declining portfolio valuations and redemptions.

3.6 Until recently, clients' losses from fraud have been small. However, recent cases have emphasized the scale of losses that investors can incur. In addition, since irregular trading is difficult to detect, it is likely that losses which clients have suffered have been substantially in excess of recorded amounts.

3.7 Losses from outright fraud may also be set to increase. Deregulation and increased competition may reduce profits and induce more financial distress. Abolition of controls on capital movements may make frauds easier to perpetrate and the perpetrators more difficult to prosecute. Chapter 4 suggested that the past levels of prosecution may not have provided adequate deterrence.

3.8 One striking observation from the past evidence is that, in the absence of fraud or theft, investor losses have been small. For example, unit trust management companies that have encountered financial difficulties have been acquired at little or no cost to investors. This suggests that, in these cases, disruption costs were low. This observation has an important bearing on the scope and design of investor protection.

Part B   Financial Failure

3.9 Some investment management firms are of above-average risk as measured by the riskiness of their equity securities. At first sight this is surprising, since investment management appears to be a relatively safe business. Risk could arise from financial gearing, but levels of gearing are comparatively low in investment management. Risk could also arise from own-positions. Position risks of investment managers of unit trusts can be appreciable, as was revealed by the survey. In the past, some unit trusts have derived around 40 per cent of their income from profits through dealing in units. This might change in the future with the introduction of a new system of pricing units. Investment positions probably exacerbated financial problems in unit trust firms in 1974/5 and contributed to large declines in income in the wake of the 1987 stock market crash.

3.10 High risks may also result from substantial fixed costs in operating an investment management business. Minimum costs of running an IM firm can be appreciable, and the ability of the firm to reduce costs in the short run following a rapid contraction of business is probably limited. This is particularly likely to be true of firms that are subject to specific rather than industry-wide dislocations.

3.11 The significance of these risks for investors depends on whether firms hold clients' balances. Losses to investors are potentially large where clients' balances are commingled with those of firm. Separation of clients' monies has therefore appreciably diminished risks to investors of financial failure.

3.12 Although, according to IMRO rules, clients' monies must be separated, some clients' funds are frequently in the temporary possession of IM firms. For example, proceeds from the sale of purchase of securities may be in the bank account of an IM manager for short periods of time. In the event of default, funds may be claimed by other creditors.

Part C   Risks in the Investment Management Process

3.13 There are three risks in the investment management process.

(a)   Small *execution errors* were by no means infrequent. They gave rise to administrative costs of correction and direct liabilities to investors. Large execution errors were uncommon, but when they occurred they could create substantial liabilities for firms. There were serious differences of view about firms' liabilities for execution errors.

(b) *Settlement delays* are common in overseas markets and were frequently encountered in UK equity markets prior to the 1987 stock market crash. The financial resources required to meet settlement delays are considerable. However, these requirements are temporary and can be met by credit facilities. In other words, they create a working capital requirement. Furthermore, settlement problems tend to be concentrated during profitable periods of buoyant activity and do not usually create serious financial problems. There was considerable uncertainty about the precise division of liability for settlement delays between investor and investment manager.

(c) Very few firms have encountered *counterparty default.* Indeed, the successful regulation of broker/dealers should limit the frequency of its occurrence. If it did occur, the survey suggested that it could create serious losses for IM firms that bore counterparty risk, particularly if default was not restricted to one counterparty. Those IM firms that were interviewed were not always clear about their liability for counterparty risk.

3.14 The implication of these observations is that large execution errors, while infrequent, present real risks to investors if IM firms default. However, those risks are not necessarily related to financial performance and should not be highly correlated across firms. Settlement delays are unlikely to cause significant failure among IM firms. On the other hand, counterparty default could do so, but only where IM firms bear this liability. Furthermore, the successful regulation of brokers and dealers should limit its occurrence.

3.15 *Of the risks resulting from asymmetric information, fraud, theft, and irregular dealing are the most serious. Pure financial risks are the least troublesome, provided that clients' balances are separated at all times. Furthermore, financial risks can be significantly diminished by placing the IM firm's own-positions in separate legal* *entities from those of the investment manager. Major execution errors present real risks to investors but are infrequent and largely unrelated to the financial performance of firms.*

SECTION 4 A Comparison of IMRO's and the Report's Responses to Risks in the IM Business

4.1 In this section IMRO's existing regulatory framework is compared with that suggested by the report.

4.2 Chapter 7 set out the thinking that has lain behind IMRO's current capital requirements. It described how attention has focused on two classes of risk faced by the investor: the risk that firms will fail to undertake the investment management process adequately, and the risk of business failure. Both risks were thought to be related to particular observable measures of the activities of firms, for example volume of business and level of expenditure. As a consequence, a degree of protection could be provided by relating capital requirements to observable measures. Two other risks, fraud and misappropriation of clients' balances, while being recognized as serious, were not thought to be appropriately corrected by capital requirements.

4.3 Capital does not therefore provide protection against the most serious form of market failure that arises in investment management, namely that owing to fraud. Chapter 7 demonstrated that capital requirements tend to provide inadequate protection of investments in small firms (where requirements are low but risks to fraud are not) and unduly onerous requirements on large firms. Furthermore, the rule that capital must exceed the maximum of that required by a firm's level of expenditure and volume of business tends to exacerbate the mismatch between risks and requirements.[1]

---

[1] The imposition of volume-of-business rules has been deferred.

4.4 The appropriate determination of capital requires detailed information on the nature of firms and the activities that they undertake. Information that has to be sought of firms includes the division of investments between gilts and equities and between domestic and overseas markets. In addition, estimates have to be provided of the relation of these activities and characteristics to the risks incurred by investors. For example, the regulator will have to be able to establish the extent to which settlement risks are affected by a reallocation of portfolios between different markets. This is complicated by the fact that the risks of operating in particular markets are dependent on the monitoring and control systems that firms employ and can alter appreciably over time as market conditions change. The survey of investment managers demonstrated that sufficiently detailed information is simply not available. The correct determination of capital will therefore place undue information requirements on both firms and regulator, will be prone to frequent revision, and will appear arbitrary to those being regulated.

4.5 These objections would be serious enough were it not for the fact that there is a more fundamental objection to the imposition of capital requirements. It has been noted above that, provided that clients' balances are separated at all times, pure financial risks are the least serious of the failures that arise in investment management. Market failures owing to asymmetric information are of much greater concern. A financial response is not appropriate for risks that relate to the integrity and ability of individuals. Furthermore, if own-positions are held in separate legal entities, systemic risks are small. Unlike banking, broking, and dealing, capital is not required to protect an economy from an industry-wide failure of investment management.

4.6 As a consequence, the form of investor protection that is proposed in this report differs in several respects from that enshrined in IMRO's rules. Table 8.1 summarizes the risks in the IM industry (cols. (1) and (2)), the proposed response (col. (3)), and the changes that are required to IMRO's rules to implement the report's proposals (col. (4)). Each category of risk is discussed in turn.

Table 8.1 A comparison of IMRO's response and the 'proposed' responses to risks in investment management

Risk (1)	IMRO's response (2)	Proposed response (3)	Suggested changes (4)
A: Fraud, irregular dealings, and misappropriation	(a) 'Fit and proper' test	(a) 'Fit and proper' test	
	(b) Conduct of business rules	(b) Conduct of business rules	
	(c) Separation of clients' balances	(c) 'Strict' separation of client balances	(c) Use of custodian for clients' assets
	(d) Inspection by IMRO and audit by private agencies	(d) Inspection by IMRO and private agencies	(d) Inspection by private agencies
	(e) SIB's limited compensation fund	(e) Full insurance	(e) Set up insurance scheme
B: Financial failure	(a) Expenditure capital requirements	(a) Private inspection	(a) Inspection by private agencies; withdraw expenditure capital requirements

	(b) Position risk capital requirements	(c) 'Strict' separation of clients' balances	(b) Withdraw position risk capital requirements (see part D)
	(c) Separation of clients' balances		(c) Use of custodian for clients' assets
	(d) SIB's limited compensation fund		
C: The investment management process	(a) Conduct-of-business rules	(a) Conduct-of-business rules	(b) Inspection by private auditor
	(b) Proposed volume-of-business rules (deferred *pro tem*)	(b) Private inspection	(c) Set up private insurance
		(c) Full private insurance	
D: Systemic risks	(a) Separation of own-positions	(a) Require legal separations of own-positions	

Part A   Fraud, Irregular Dealings, and Misappropriation

4.7   IMRO's response to these risks has been five-fold. First, it has imposed a 'fit and proper' test on those entering the industry and holding senior positions in IM firms. This test is performed on application to IMRO and periodically thereafter. Second, each firm is subject to 'conduct-of-business' rules which, for example, regulate the nature and wording of contracts between the IM firm and its clients. Third, existing rules require cash balances to be separated from those of the firm. Fourth, inspections are undertaken by IMRO either with 'prior' notice or in 'surprise' visits. Finally, the SIB has established a compensation fund for investor losses, with annual payments limited to £100 million for all SROs.

4.8   *The report's proposed response for Part A risks is similar to IMRO's but with three specific differences. It has been suggested that IMRO might delegate additional inspection responsibilities to the private auditors of IM firms.* For example, in the USA the SEC requires each firm's auditors to conduct surprise inspections of IM firms each year to reconcile clients' assets. It may be that UK auditors can substitute for some monitoring currently undertaken by IMRO. This is particularly important in cases in which IM firms hold clients' balances (licensed deposit-takers) or clients' securities. Where IM firms are not licensed deposit-takers, the report recommends that *clients' assets should be strictly separated from those of the ·IM firm.* Thus, client cash balances and securities should be under the control of a (third-party) custodian. Strict separation is already a feature of unit trusts (where the trustee acts as a custodian), and explains why investor losses have been so low in the unit trust business. We believe that this measure would significantly diminish the risk of fraud. Even if strict separation is not imposed on the whole industry, it should be imposed on those firms newly entering the industry without an established reputation. Elsewhere disclosure specifying whether custodians hold individual client bank accounts and securities may be adequate. Finally, it is suggested that a *full insurance fund be established for IMRO members.*

4.9 The report compares the advantages and disadvantages of mutual private insurance. There are some advantages in employing the monitor (in this case IMRO) as the insurer. This encourages a high standard of monitoring by forcing the monitor to bear the consequence of failures. In addition, private insurance will involve some duplication of the monitoring undertaken by IMRO. On the other hand, private provision introduces competition into the pricing of insurance. Furthermore, the mutual insurer may be under more political pressure than private insurers to subsidize certain segments of the industry. The choice between mutual and private insurance is a difficult one and will require further investigation.

Part B   Risks of Financial Failure

4.10 IMRO's response has been to impose capital requirements based on expenditure and the size of own-positions. Clients' balances are separated to prevent client funds from becoming general creditors of the firm in the event of failure. Finally, SIB's compensation fund is available for liabilities arising from failure (subject to stipulated limitations).

4.11 The response proposed in this report is substantially different. *Capital requirements should not be used to provide protection against these risks. Both expenditure and position risk capital requirements should be withdrawn once the other recommendations of the report have been implemented.* (But see Part D in relation to systemic risk.) Since the risks of financial failure affect individual firms rather than the industry, capital is a costly and inefficient form of protection. Any market failures arising from inadequate information can be better neutralized by strengthening the responsibilities of private auditing firms. Still more significantly, *'strict' separation of client balances should be required*, so that if failure occurs, clients' monies caught in the transmission process will not become part of the pool of funds available to creditors.

4.12 It might be thought that the abolition of capital requirements will weaken the regulator's discretionary powers to intervene in the activities of the IM firm. The violation of a capital requirement rule may be used by the regulator to justify intensified monitoring where impending financial failure is suspected. Bond covenants serve similar purposes in transactions between borrowers and lenders. However, capital requirements are not the appropriate vehicle for creating those powers. The imposition of capital requirements on an entire industry for the purpose of monitoring a few firms is unduly costly. Moreover, well established techniques based on accounting and market-based data are available for identifying high-risk firms. IMRO could usefully explore the application of formal techniques of financial modelling to the monitoring process.

Part C   Risks Arising in the Investment Management Process

4.13   IMRO's response to these risks has been the imposition of business rules and capital requirements based on the volume of business. The latter has, however, been deferred *pro tem* (in an instruction dated September 1988).

4.14   It is recognized that IM firms may not exercise adequate care in undertaking certain investment management activities, for example the execution and settlement of transactions. However, *capital is not an appropriate response to these risks*, because the risks are not correlated with financial performance, and are largely uncorrelated across firms. The report's proposal is to *supplement conduct-of-business rules with private insurance. The functions of the private auditor should be strengthened* to ensure that errors in execution and settlement are detected and compensation is paid to clients where appropriate.

Part D   Systemic Risks

4.15   Prima facie systemic risks do not appear to have played a major part in the design of IMRO's rule book. However, capital requirements may have reduced systemic risks by reducing the probability of default of individual firms.

4.16 Provided that clients' balances and securities are separated from those of IM firms' own accounts, in the absence of fraud, assets of failed IM firms will be saleable. As a result, disruption costs to investors will be low. Should systemic risks, such as a stock market crash, cause IM failures, it should be possible for the assets of these firms to be absorbed elsewhere. However, should the regulatory authority attach greater significance to systemic risks, then the most effective protection is for the regulator to require that *firms' own investments be held separately from the legal entity that manages investors' funds. The result of strict separation of clients' monies and assets from the firms' own investments will be a pure investment management firm with a substantially lower risk of financial failure.*

4.7 To summarize, the recommendations in this report are designed to protect investors against market failures. The most important failures concern fraud, irregular dealings, misappropriation, and inadequate execution of the investment management process. Financial failures and systemic risks are of less significance. As a consequence, the report recommends that

(a)   existing capital requirements be abolished;
(b)   third-party custodians be used to protect clients' monies and securities;
(c)   full insurance be provided to investors;
(d)   investments by firms on their own accounts be kept in separate legal entities from investment management.

4.18 In addition, the report suggests that

(a)   clarification is needed about the liability of firms for execution and settlement problems in the investment management process;
(b)   the possibility of delegating some of IMRO's monitoring functions to private auditors should be explored;
(c)   in determining appropriate levels of protection, a distinction may be drawn between private and institutional investors; for example, monitoring and auditing may be adequate for

institutional investors, but insurance may be required for individual investors.

4.19   Finally, the report noted the following.

(a)   Irregular dealing and unreported fraud may be significant. Conduct-of-business rules (regarding, for example, the pricing of units in unit trusts) play an important role in discouraging such activites. So too do effective methods of detecting, prosecuting, and penalizing fraud and theft.

(b)   Companies that have been set up to defraud tend to have low levels of initial capital, to operate for short periods, to employ hard selling techniques, and to take own-positions; furthermore, they do not strictly separate clients' accounts from those of the firm.

(c)   Formal tools of financial modelling can be used to identify firms that are vulnerable to failure without requiring the imposition of capital requirements.

(d)   US regulation of investment managers displays many of the features proposed in this report. In particular, it places little emphasis on capital as a form of protection, requires explicit authorization from clients for investment managers to have custody of funds and securities, and emphasizes disclosure, the role of the public accountant, and the imposition of *ex post* penalites in protecting clients against loss.

SECTION 5   Costs and Benefits of Proposed Changes

5.1   In Table 8.2 the costs and benefits of the proposed changes are outlined. We discuss each in turn.

Part A   Elimination of Capital Requirements

5.2   Most IM firms' holdings of capital far exceeded IMRO's requirements. It is possible that IMRO's requirements are set below the minimum capital perceived by IM firms as being necessary to operate the business. Alternatively, capital is held well above IMRO's minimum requirements to avoid risks of violating the rules. In the former case IMRO's capital requirements are costless but probably ineffective; in the latter, they may be very costly.

5.3 The major objection that can be raised against the elimination of capital requirements is that the incidence of default may increase as a consequence. If capital requirements are binding, this possibility cannot be ruled out. However, provided that investors are fully protected against losses by a combination of insurance and strict separation of clients' balances, then it is not the proper role of the regulator to prevent such defaults. The assertion that defaults are simply unacceptable does not accord with the observations that they are not only tolerated elsewhere but are even sometimes cited as a sign of the healthy functioning of market processes.

5.4 Where capital requirements are binding, their elimination will reduce capital costs. This will be particularly important for firms that have poor access to capital markets, primarily small and new firms. As a consequence, barriers to the entry of new firms into the industry will be diminished and competition intensified. More generally, lower costs should be reflected in lower prices of services provided and improved international competitiveness of the UK IM industry. In an industry in which firms are highly mobile between countries, even fairly small deviations from optimal regulatory arrangements can have serious consequences.

Part B   Strict Separation of Clients' Monies

5.5 There may be some extra costs arising from the strict separation of clients' monies. We were not led to believe that those costs would be large. However, there would be substantial benefits arising from lower levels of fraud and reduced costs to investors of financial distress.

Table 8.2 Costs and benefits of the proposed changes

Change in regulation	Costs		Benefits	
I: Elimination of capital requirements	(i)	Political implications in the event of a default	(i)	Reduced costs of holding capital if capital requirements are binding
	(ii)	Disruption costs arising from more defaults if capital requirements are binding	(ii)	Reduced barriers to entry
II: Strict separation of clients' monies	(i)	Custodian function	(i)	Lower level of fraud
			(ii)	Fewer bankruptcies affecting investors
			(iii)	Smaller costs of bankruptcy to the investor

III: Insurance	(i)	Direct costs of running an insurance scheme	(i)	Protection against losses arising from fraud
	(ii)	Costs arising from inefficiencies in an insurance market	(ii)	Protection against failures in the IM process
IV: Separation of own-positions	(i)	Administrative costs of running own-positions in separate legal entities	(i)	Lower incidence of failure and lower disruption costs
			(ii)	Reduced systemic risks

Part C   Insurance

5.6   There are two costs associated with running a full insurance scheme. First, there are the direct administrative costs. These have to be set against some of the costs of running current regulatory arrrangements. Second, there are costs arising from inefficiencies in insurance markets. These reflect difficulties in distinguishing between low- and high-quality firms. In some cases, these problems prevent the emergence of insurance markets altogether. Therefore it may be necessary to make recourse to mutual insurance to provide protection against fraud, irregular dealings, and misappropriation. The benefits in terms of enhanced investor protection would be substantial.

Part D   Separation of Own-Positions

5.7   We were not led to believe that the administrative costs of separating own-positions would be high. The benefits are that it will reduce the level of failures and therefore disruption costs in the IM business. Furthermore, systemic risks will be diminished.

Part E   Overall Costs and Benefits

5.8   Any estimate of the overall costs and benefits must await detailed discussions with interested parties such as insurers and custodians. However, the benefits promise full protection for investors, reduced risks of fraud, and more competition.

5.9   By providing full investor protection, the regulatory authority may have less to fear from IM companies failing and leaving the industry. This may make for a simpler regulatory system.

References

Aghion, P. and Bolton, P. (1988), 'An Incomplete Contract Approach to Bankruptcy and the Financial Structure of the Firm'. Mimeo.

Akerlof, G. A. (1970), 'The Market for "Lemons": Quality Uncertainty and the Market Mechanism', *Quarterly Journal of Economics*, 84: 488–500.

Altman, E. A. (1983), *Corporate Financial Distress: A Complete Guide to Predicting, Avoiding and Dealing with Bankruptcy*. New York: John Wiley.

Battacharya, S. (1979), 'Imperfect Information Dividend Policy and "The Bird in the Hand" Fallacy', *Bell Journal of Economics*, 10: 259–70.

Brealey, R. A. and Myers, S. C. (1988), *Principles of Finance* (3rd edn.). Maidenhead, Berks: McGraw-Hill.

Diamond, D. W. and Dybvig, P. H. (1983), 'Bank Runs, Deposit Insurance and Liquidity', *Journal of Political Economy*, 91: 401–19.

Edwards, J. S. (1984), 'Does Dividend Policy Matter?' *Fiscal Studies*, 5: 1–17.

Grossman, S. J. and Hart, O. D. (1982), 'Corporate Financial Structure and Managerial Incentives', in J. McCall (ed.), *The Economics of Information and Uncertainty*. Chicago: NBER.

Jensen, M. C. and Meckling, W. H. (1976), 'Theory of the Firm: Managerial Behaviour, Agency Costs and Ownership Structure', *Journal of Financial Economics*, 3: 305–60.

John, K. and Williams, J. (1985), 'Dividends, Dilution and Taxes: A Signalling Equilibrium', *Journal of Finance*, 40: 1053–70.

Kareken, J. H. (1986), 'Federal Bank Regulatory Policy: A Description and Some Observations', *Journal of Business*, 59: 3–48.

Leland, H. E. (1979), 'Quacks, Lemons and Licensing: A Theory of Minimum Quality Standards', *Journal of Political Economy*, 87: 1328–46.

Mayer, C. P. (1989), 'Finance and Investment: A Real Relationship'. Mimeo.

Miller, M. H. and Rock, K. (1985), 'Dividend Policy under Asymmetric Information', *Journal of Finance*, 40: 1031–51.

Modigliani, F. and Miller, M. H. (1958), 'The Cost of Capital Corporation Finance and the Theory of Investment', *American Economic Review*, 48: 161–97.

—— (1963), 'Corporate Income Taxes and the Cost of Capital: A Correction', *American Economic Review*, 53: 433–43.

—— (1969), 'Reply to Heins and Sprenkle', *American Economic Review*, 59: 592–5.

Ross, S. A. (1977), 'The Determination of Financial Structure: The Incentive-signalling Approach', *Bell Journal of Economics*, 7: 23–40.

Santomero, A. M. and Watson, R. D. (1977), 'Determining an Optimal Capital Standard for the Banking Industry', *Journal of Finance*, 32: 1267–82.

Schaefer, S. (1987), 'The Design of Bank Regulation and Supervision; Some Lessons from the Theory of Finance', in R. Portes and A. Swoboda (eds.), *Threats to International Financial Stability*. Cambridge University Press.

Shaked, A. and Sutton, J. (1981), 'The Self-regulating Professions', *Review of Economic Studies*, 48: 217–34.

Shapiro, C. (1986), 'Investment, Moral Hazard and Occupational Licensing', *Review of Economic Studies*, 53: 843–62.

Stiglitz, J. E. (1969), 'A Re-examination of the Modigliani–Miller Theorem', *American Economic Review*, 59: 851–66.

—— (1974), 'On the Irrelevance of Corporate Financial Policy', *American Economic Review*, 64: 851–5.

—— and Weiss, A. (1981), 'Credit Rationing in Markets with Imperfect Information', *American Economic Review*, 71: 393–410.

Index